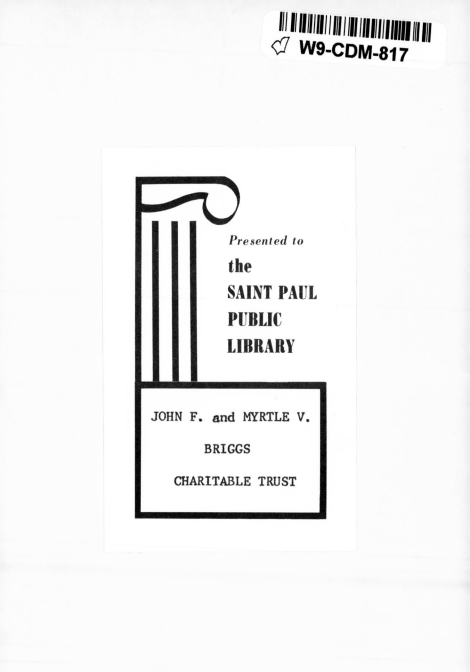

Twayne's United States Author's Series

Sylvia E. Bowman, *Editor*

INDIANA UNIVERSITY

Edwin O'Connor

Hans Namuth

EDWIN O'CONNOR

EDWIN O'CONNOR

By HUGH RANK
Governors State University

Twayne Publishers, Inc. ::   New York

Library of Congress Cataloging in Publication Data

Rank, Hugh.
  Edwin O'Connor.

  (Twayne's United States authors series, TUSAS 242)
  Bibliography: p.
  1. O'Connor, Edwin.
PS3565.C55Z85   813'.5'4   73-17301
ISBN 0-8057-0555-4

To Lee
Ubi caritas . . .

But you asked me what writers I admire. Well, the only American fiction writers I always read are Salinger, James Baldwin, Edwin O'Connor.

EDMUND WILSON
The Bit Between My Teeth

Preface

If much of this first full length study of Edwin O'Connor seems to take the form of a "corrective introduction," such correction is necessary. The extent of O'Connor's achievement has been concealed, ironically, by his own subtlety in craftsmanship and by his complexity of vision. Fervent Irishmen, for example, read *The Last Hurrah* and rejoiced in its Gaelic exuberance without recognizing its detached, sometimes cynical, view of the Irish in America. Pious Catholics read *The Edge of Sadness* because it was a novel about a priest, and they were exposed to the most penetrating criticism of the American priesthood ever written. Nevertheless, the general reading public found something in O'Connor's works which delighted them; and perhaps this very fact of his popular success has caused some literary and academic critics to assume, illogically, that nothing of "literary merit" could be found in these novels which had such widespread popular appeal.

Thus, *The Last Hurrah* has been dismissed as a thinly disguised *roman à clef* about Boston's Mayor James Michael Curley (which it isn't); *All in the Family*, a *roman à clef* about the Kennedys (which it isn't); and *The Edge of Sadness,* a story about the cantankerous Charlie Carmody (which it isn't). In fact, half of the published reviews of this last-mentioned novel didn't even correctly identify the *protagonist* of the story; these reviewers naively accepted the narrator's disclaimer ("This story is not my own.") and missed the major conflict of that excellent novel. Repeatedly, the published reviews about O'Connor's work abound in errors of fact or in gross misinterpretations.

While researching for this study, I met graduate students who had sought to write about O'Connor; but they had been discouraged by their academic advisors who told them to avoid the subject because "nothing has been written on him." Such topsy-turvy logic reflects a common attitude in American scholarship today when competent graduate students are urged to write the 501st dissertation about William Faulkner and to avoid "unknown" authors. While there is some value in training an academic cadre of Faulkner-Melville-James experts, the recent revolution in Black Studies has demonstrated that there are thousands of "unknown" writers in American literature, some of whom produced works of genuine merit.

My purpose in this study of O'Connor is to provide an introduction to a writer who has been generally ignored by academic critics despite his extraordinary popular reception and his artistic recognition as a Pulitzer Prize winner. Hopefully, this study will bring more attention to O'Connor's three major novels about the Irish experience in America, novels that chronicle the changing generations and their relationship to politics, church, and family: *The Last Hurrah, The Edge of Sadness,* and *All in the Family.* Of these, I consider *The Edge of Sadness* to be the best artistically, and also to be one of the truly distinguished novels in modern American literature. By pointing out some of O'Connor's themes and techniques, readers may be stimulated to read, or re-read, these novels in order to form their own evaluations.

Biographical material about O'Connor's early life and apprentice period is contained in the first two chapters. Succeeding chapters open with the relevant biographical background for his later years; the final section within these chapters summarizes the critical response of the reviewers. The mid-sections within the chapters are devoted to a close reading of the texts themselves. Since O'Connor's fiction has been criticized as being "rambling," "loose," or "not coherent," such an extensive explication is especially necessary to demonstrate the coherence of the novels, the interwoven plots, the "detour" style of the storyteller, the function of the many anecdotes and "comic grotesque" characters, and the important role of the narrator.

I was aided in my work through the courtesy of Richard Matsek, the librarian of Sacred Heart University, by Angela Guglielmo and Marion Cahill, and by Dan Bernd, my colleague at Governors State University. In addition, I am indebted to the hospitality of O'Connor's family and friends, who kindly consented to being interviewed: Veniette O'Connor (his widow); Mrs. John V. O'Connor (his mother); Mr. and Mrs. William Burrell (his sister and brother-in-law); Mr. Arthur Gartland; Mr. George Hall; Professor John V. Kelleher; Mr. Robert Manning;

Preface

Professor Arthur Schlesinger, Jr.; Mr. Joseph Vitale; Mr. Edward Weeks; and, especially, Mrs. Esther Yntema, a senior editor at the Atlantic Monthy Press, who helped in so many ways. Permission to quote published materials has been granted by the Atlantic Monthly Press; permission to quote from the unpublished manuscripts has been granted by Veniette O'Connor. Naturally, the interpretaton of factual material gathered from these sources is my own.

HUGH RANK

Governors State University
Park Forest South, Illinois

Contents

Chronology

1918   Edwin Greene O'Connor born in Providence, Rhode Island, on July 29; parents, Dr. John V. and Mary Greene O'Connor.

1918–   Lived in Woonsocket, Rhode Island. Trip to Hollywood,
1935   California, with his father in 1928. Attended LaSalle Academy in Providence, 1931–35.

1935–   University of Notre Dame, Indiana. As an English major,
1939   he met Professor Frank O'Malley, an important life-long influence. Returned (September–November, 1939) for brief stay in graduate school.

1940–   Worked as a radio announcer at stations in Providence,
1942   Rhode Island; Palm Beach, Florida; Buffalo, New York; and Hartford, Connecticut. Frequent submissions, but no publications, of satirical sketches.

1942–   Joined Coast Guard. Stationed in Boston, Cape Cod, Balti-
1945   more, and Boston again where he worked under Louis Brems, former Boston city greeter and vaudeville actor, source of political folklore. Wrote autobiographical "Coast Guard" manuscript.

1945–   Returned to radio work; a year as a writer-announcer for
1946   Boston station of the Yankee network.

1946   Started free-lance writing as sole income. *Atlantic* published his first series of satires on radio.

1946–   Stories and articles, mostly unpublished. Two novels at-
1950   tempted: "Luther Sudworth" and "Anthony Cantwell." Started spending summers at Wellfleet on Cape Cod.

1951   *The Oracle*, rejected by Atlantic, published by Harpers.

1952   "A Young Man of Promise" novel-manuscript written and then withheld as he begins work on *The Last Hurrah*.

1953   January: near-fatal ulcer hemorrhage; March, first visit to Ireland. Work continued on *The Last Hurrah* and as editor of Fred Allen's scripts for *Treadmill to Oblivion*.

1954   Second trip to Ireland with Fred Allen and Portland Hoffa.

1955   *The Last Hurrah* submitted in January: won Atlantic Prize in March. Continued work with Fred Allen on *Much Ado About Me.*

1956   *The Last Hurrah* published in February; four hard-cover printings within the month; fifteen by October. June, invited to Notre Dame commencement; September, father died; O'Connor took mother to Atlantic City afterward, inspired to write *Benjy.*

1957   Pulitzer Prize committee announced deadlock; no prize awarded in fiction for previous year. *Benjy* published.

1958   Movie of *The Last Hurrah* released. Trip to Rome to witness ceremonies as Pope John XXIII made a Cardinal of Boston's Archbishop Cushing.

1961   *The Edge of Sadness* published. Met Veniette Caswell Weil at Wellfleet.

1962   Pulitzer Prize awarded to *The Edge of Sadness* in May; married Veniette, September 2.

1964   *I Was Dancing*, first written as a play; then revised into novel form, was published as a novel in March; ran on Broadway in November for seventeen performances.

1966   *All in the Family* published.

1967   Working on *The Traveler from Brazil* (play); completed, but not staged.

1968   Returned to fiction. Worked on "Cardinal" manuscript and was working on the "Boy" manuscript when he died of a cerebral hemorrhage, March 23.

1970   Posthumous publication of *The Best and the Last of Edwin O'Connor.*

CHAPTER 1

The Early Years

I *Childhood and Youth*

EDWIN GREENE O'CONNOR, who was born in Providence, Rhode Island, on July 29, 1918, was the first child of Doctor John V. and Mary Greene O'Connor. His father, formerly a pharmacist, had earlier sold his drug store in order to go to medical school. After graduation in 1911, Doctor O'Connor interned and practiced for five years before getting married. Following graduate studies at Johns Hopkins and Harvard, Doctor O'Connor returned to his hometown of Woonsocket, Rhode Island, as a specialist in internal medicine. Edwin O'Connor's mother was a graduate of Rhode Island Normal and had taught school for three years prior to her marriage. At the insistence of her husband, she stopped teaching and did not resume her career until forty years later, after her husband's death.

Doctor O'Connor was a powerful, self-made man. Although not the oldest in his own large family of nine children, he did become the patriarch of the clan through the sheer force of his personality. He was dominant, a perfectionist in many regards, and highly competent; not only was he considered one of New England's finest specialists, but also he had been elected by his colleagues as president of the local medical society. Within his community, within the clan, and within the immediate family, Doctor O'Connor was a leader and an authority.

Three other children were born to the O'Connors: in 1922, an infant daughter lived only four days, then John was born in 1923, and Barbara in 1928. Since Edwin was five years older than his brother and ten years older than his sister, this age spread should be noted. The children were not close playmates and this may account for the "only child" feeling which is evident in some of O'Connor's later writings about boyhood.

Despite his parents and the large number of aunts and uncles, all of whom were second-generation immigrant stock, Edwin O'Connor did not grow up in a conspicuously "Irish" household such as might be found in the ethnic-oriented families of a big city ghetto. The O'Connors, as a doctor's family, were rather well to do, lived in a "better" section of suburban Woonsocket, and were rather isolated from other relatives who had also moved out into a wider society. Most of the "Irishness" in O'Connor's novels was drawn, therefore, from his observations later as an adult and not from his childhood memories. However, a few of the relatives may have been the genesis for certain character relationships or the source of anecdotes or ideas. For example, O'Connor's Uncle Tom, a minor politician in Woonsocket, possibly inspired the Knocko Minihan wake scene which appeared first in "De Mortuis" and which was eventually incorporated into *The Last Hurrah*. His uncle, Edwin George O'Connor, for whom O'Connor was named, had been in the theater all of his life, from vaudeville to movies. One of O'Connor's most memorable experiences from boyhood was a trip to California in 1928, alone with his father, to visit his uncle, James Greene, who was then a technical director for the Hal Roach Studio; photos from this trip show the young Edwin playing with the cast of the "Our Gang" comedies. Throughout his life, O'Connor remained fascinated with vaudevillians (*I Was Dancing*), the theater, and the movies.

Because he had attended the public elementary school, Edwin's family thought he ought to have some religious schooling at the secondary level. Thus, in 1931, he entered LaSalle Academy in Providence, a parochial boys' school run by the Christian Brothers. Commuting daily from Woonsocket, he took the standard Classical course (four years of Latin, three years of Greek), was president of the Latin Club, and was also active in dramatics. Although tall and athletic, he was unable to report for the baseball or basketball teams because of his daily commuting routine. But he did try out for the cross-country team, an adventure he twice recalled in interviews as being a failure: he placed sixty-second in his first meet and eighty-third in his second and last attempt.

II *Notre Dame*

During high school, O'Connor had not given much thought about going to college, but in his senior year a Holy Cross missionary priest from Notre Dame preached an extended "mission" service at O'Connor's parish church. Apparently impressed, O'Connor applied to the University of Notre Dame with only a vague notion about why he wanted to go to college or why to one so far from home. "I didn't know a soul there," he said later in a *Boston Post* interview of February 13, 1956; "I don't know to this day why I chose Notre Dame. I just thought I'd like to go there, and that was all right with my father. I'm delighted Notre Dame accepted me. I love the place." His experience at Notre Dame changed his life; and he remained, throughout his life, deeply influenced by the men and the ideas he encountered there.

In the 1930's, a generation before Father Hesburgh's campaign for "intellectual excellence" began, Notre Dame was more noted for its leadership in athletics than in academics. The "Fighting Irish" had long dominated the national football scene, and millions of American Catholics were loyal "subway alumni" who cheered for the school which in some way symbolized their struggles and aspirations. On campus, students led a Spartan life of rigid discipline in the dormitories and classrooms. Notre Dame's dual function, it seems, was to indoctrinate students in the faith and to prepare these second- and third-generation immigrant children for jobs in business, teaching, and civil service. Despite this generally pragmatic and conservative orientation of the college, the English Department was noteworthy not only for its liberal tendencies but also for a remarkable collection of charismatic teachers. Best described in terms of "Christian Humanists," teachers such as John T. Frederick, Richard Sullivan, and Father Leo L. Ward (all of whom were active writers) gave the department a special vitality and offered students men of great personal warmth, creative abiilty, and professional competency as models for adult male behavior.

One teacher, Frank O'Malley, had a special influence on O'Connor: "the greatest single help for me in college." As a student in O'Malley's freshman course in composition, O'Connor was steered away from a journalism major in favor of English. Later, O'Connor took O'Malley's "Modern Catholic Writers" course, a distinguished series of lectures or meditations about the relation of literature and faith. Long famous at Notre Dame as a course which attracted crowds of drop-in auditors, O'Malley's lectures had a widespread influence on scores of students who have subsequently been active on all levels of writing and editorial work. A feature story in *Time* of February 9, 1962, for example, commented about this course: "Perhaps no one else has better conveyed that sense [of a Christian view of man] to Notre Dame students than witty, incisive English Professor Frank O'Malley, 28 years on the faculty and the University's most inspiring undergraduate teacher. O'Malley plumbs life's most basic emotions, using Charles Peguy to examine the virtue of hope, Claudel to plumb suffering, Kierkegaard to emphasize the shallowness of religion without love. When he reaches students, O'Malley often changes their lives, teaching them to love learning and learn love" (p. 54). The friendship between O'Connor and O'Malley endured. In later years, O'Connor as an alumnus was not one to attend football games or local alumni meetings, but every year for over a decade O'Connor returned to Notre Dame for a week or so to visit O'Malley, to read manuscripts to him, and to lecture in his course. In 1962, the prize-winning book, *The Edge of Sadness*, was dedicated to Frank O'Malley.

But the college years at Notre Dame were not confined only to the classroom. O'Connor was an active undergraduate both in his studies (English major, philosophy minor, Bachelor of Arts *cum laude*) and in extracurricular activity. In his first two years, he played baseball, primarily as a reserve pitcher—usually accompanied by the team chanting "Allah, Allah" in reference to his elaborate wind-up motion which struck them as being similar to a Moslem at prayer. O'Connor was also an announcer at the campus radio station and a regular contributor to the literary magazine. One of his early stories published in *Scrip* in November, 1938, was ironically titled "Friends are Made at McCabes" in which the college-graduate narrator relates a controlled, understated story of the breakup of the friendship of two of his companions when one steals the other's girlfriend; underneath the obvious triangle conflict, the friction of Irish-Italian antagonism is deftly suggested. This awareness of ethnic differences apparently developed in this period. In an interview (*New York Herald Tribune*, February 2, 1956, p. 2) after *The Last Hurrah*, O'Connor mentioned this influence from his classmates, sons of Chicago politicians, and the visits to their homes where he sought out older people to listen to their conversations: "I'd open an avenue for them to discuss politics and then sit back and listen. I'd take careful note of everything they said. I'd put it down in a notebook later."

By his senior year, O'Connor had decided to be a writer. His record at that time was scanty—a few publications in his home-town newspaper and six or seven rejection slips from national magazines—but his determination was set. When O'Connor announced his decision to Father Leo L. Ward, head of the English Department, O' Connor was given the advice that he'd starve to death unless he found a job in which he'd have the spare time to write. After graduation, he was still unsure of what to do; and he returned on a scholarship to Notre Dame's graduate school in the following September. By mid-November, he realized that the graduate program was not geared for the creative writer, so he dropped out of graduate school to begin looking for a job. "No one, least of all myself," wrote O'Connor in the "Coast Guard" manuscript a few years later, "seemed exactly certain of the proper method for tackling this fateful future, for I was a Bachelor of Arts. Had I been a Civil Engineer or Pre-Medical student, I should have known long beforehand that my days were to be forever occupied with suspension bridges or appendectomies, but a Liberal Arts student was afforded no such precise security."

CHAPTER 2

The Apprenticeship

WITH the spectacular reception of *The Last Hurrah* in 1956, Edwin O'Connor achieved a reputation, erroneously, of being an "overnight success." Despite local interviews and brief notes which made some mention of his background in radio, the general popular attitude (reflected, too, in many published comments) was that O'Connor as a writer had had a "lucky" break with his "first" novel. While it is true that he did go from obscurity to national prominence within a few weeks, this part of the Cinderella story tends to neglect the long years of apprenticeship which he served. O'Connor's apprentice work not only refutes this misconception, but also indicates certain typical themes and patterns of his early unpublished writings which will also appear in his more mature publications. Although very few of O'Connor's unpublished manuscripts are dated, approximate dates can often be estimated by his street address which frequently appeared on the title page.

I *Radio and Rejection Slips*

Early in 1940, O'Connor joined radio station WPRO in Providence as an announcer. Although his deep, resonant voice was a distinct asset for him in this job, his independence and sense of good taste eventually worked against a career in this field. "The first commercial announcement I read over the air," O'Connor related in the "Coast Guard" manuscript, "was a powerful appeal to all women who were in dire need of hosiery. 'Ladies!' it began, 'How are your legs?' This abrupt question always struck me as overly familiar, and I could never read it without a feeling of deep embarrassment. My employer, whose duty it was to notice such things, told me that the trick was to strike a happy medium between absolute indifference and lechery." O'Connor also recalled that later he would come across "similarly-phrased bits of commercial copy, and I quaked whenever I read them."

During the next two years, he traded positions with a radio announcer in West Palm Beach; later he moved to a Buffalo station (where he was fired for "insubordination" when he protested against a virtual dawn-to-midnight shift), then to Hartford. In this period, he was writing short stories; but, despite his submissions through an agent, nothing sold. The extant manuscripts from his Hartford address are all brief satirical sketches: "Where Do You Hail From?" (12 pp.) is a radio script satirizing commercials, which was written hopefully for the Fred Allen show; written in November, 1941, it indicates O'Connor's early admiration for Allen. "Oh No You Don't, George Jean" (7 pp.) , a light satire, alludes to a remark in Nathan's *The Bachelor* about color-coordinated cosmetics; the agent's comment on the rejection slip urged O'Connor to "keep it up" as he almost had the *"New Yorker* touch." *"My* Most Unforgettable Character" (6 pp.) was apparently written for the *Reader's Digest* as a parody of their feature article; his agent's note sternly informed him that this magazine would never consider such a piece. "The Man From the Arctic" (5 pp.) presents a rambling storyteller, a wildly eccentric Arctic explorer, who relates his adventures in a string of imitation Perelman jokes. "Literary Tea" (5 pp.) satirizes the shoptalk of the "dreary people," a fellowship of professors and old ladies, who write childrens' books. "Hello There, Sweetness and Light!" (5 pp.) is a sophomoric parody filled with pretentious literary allusions and zany *non sequitur* asides.

Although these early writing projects failed, these years were important for O'Connor's development as a writer because the radio experience trained and disciplined his attention to dialogue and speech patterns. Here, as Edward Weeks has said, O'Connor "learned to write with his ears." In addition, O'Connor's satiric insight deepened as he was daily saturated with a flood of words, yet kept a critical perspective because he had an insider's view of how radio really worked.

II *The "Coast Guard" Manuscript*

When the war started, O'Connor tried to enlist in the army, but he was rejected because of poor vision. A few months later, he enlisted in the Coast Guard in which he served for three years. The "Coast Guard" manuscript (156 pages in 26 chapters) was written in the summer of 1943; the opening chapters of this autobiographical narrative relate incidents in his early life, but most of the manuscript tells of his first year in the service. As such, it is one of the probable thousands of unpublished manuscripts written by young men about their adventures or comic misadventures in the military. Scores of these stories (such as *See Here Private Hargrove*,) were published in the war years detailing the humorous side of the military—the misfit in the organization, the breakdown of the system, the ludicrous human comedy of civilians thrust into uniform. In this *genre*, O'Connor's manuscript is certainly an above-average one; it is filled with good reading, humorous incidents, rich details; and all are narrated in a lighthearted, breezy style.

As a recruit, O'Connor's defense of his country began in Boston where the basic trainees were housed in the overcrowded Brunswick Hotel (twelve bunks to a double room) and where they drilled on Boston Common. Afterwards, he was sent to Cape Cod, deserted by its usual tourists, where he spent the next year patrolling the lonely beaches waiting for Hitler to attack: "we would slog along for hours in the soft sand, like Laurel and Hardy lost in the desert." Interesting characters, such as Greek dancers and "con" men, attracted his attention; but the routine was generally boring, broken only by weekend movies ("the aging of Jane Withers" as he described them) or occasional leaves to New York City, where he watched the radio broadcasts of his favorite comedian, Fred Allen. Transferred to Boston, he entered Chemical Warfare School there, then was sent to Baltimore for additional training in this subject. After completing the advanced course, he returned to Boston to give instruction in gas-mask techniques to the men on the incoming ships. He taught under severe handicaps since he had to bellow above the noise of ships' repair to an audience of men eager for shore leave.

The manuscript ends at this point, but the most important factor in O'Connor's Coast Guard experience occurred during the next two years. Transferred to the Public Information Office in Boston, O'Connor became a friend of his superior officer, Lieutenant Louis J. Brems, a former vaudeville performer who had worked for years, under Mayor Maurice Tobin, as Boston's official greeter.

As such, Brems was the intimate of many leading politicians and was a delightful raconteur who constantly told humorous stories, often in dialect, of the political events and personalities of city politics in Boston, Chicago, New York, Jersey City, Detroit, and Philadelphia. O'Connor was intrigued by the flamboyant Brems, who showered him with anecdotes which formed the basic source of material for *The Last Hurrah*. At the time, O'Connor was not consciously planning that novel, but he did absorb and retain much of what Brems said. In the novel, the character of Cuke Gillen is patterned after Louis Brems, but Brems' influence as a storyteller was far greater than his role as a character model.

III *The "Anthony Cantwell" Fragments*

Three fragments exist of an intended novel about "Anthony Cantwell." Portions of these manuscripts are typed on the reverse side of old mimeographed scripts from the Coast Guard Information Office; thus, these works were probably written about 1945 while O'Connor was still in the service. The first two fragments appear to be drafts of an opening chapter; but, because they present two distinct, and contradictory, movements, it appears that O'Connor was making his initial probes with more desire to write *something* rather than to tell a specific story. In one of these brief drafts, titled "Prologue" (9 pp.), Sergeant Anthony Cantwell is preparing to leave the small, deserted Pacific island where he and two other Americans, a bedraggled major and a sullen Negro private, have been stationed for three years as the sole "occupation forces." Anthony is eager to leave, but he doesn't know what he is going to do in civilian life. In the other short draft, titled "The Book" (11 pp.), the opening pages repeat the descriptions of the island's jungle scenery, but the major tells Anthony that Washington has finally remembered their existence and is planning to send more soldiers to the lonely island. The conflict between the major and the private gets more attention, and the impending "visitors" seem to constitute a threat to their lethargic, lax life. In contrast to the other draft, it seems that the action, if this story were continued, was to occur on the island.

The third "Anthony Cantwell" fragment, untitled, is much longer (79 pp. extant) and shows a definite grasp of a plot situation. As it opens, Anthony Cantwell, a month after his discharge from the service, is addressed by his father, Jonathan, who tells him that he has "good news." Anthony winces, remembering the times in the past when his father announced "good news": the music lessons arranged for him by his father, the boxing lessons his father forced him to take, and the enlistment in the army which his father, outraged by Anthony's apathy, had maneuvered despite Anthony's draft-exempt status. Now, once more, he faced "the grim benevolence" of his father who has just arranged for the jobless Anthony to begin teaching at Saint Mansard, a college in Indiana. Anthony, months ago while still on a Pacific island, had rehearsed a brave role for an anticipated confrontation scene; but he is now cowed by his father's command. The father tells Anthony that the job was secured through the political influence of his friend, Senator Mayhew.

After his father leaves, Anthony is in despair. He doesn't want to teach, and once again he feels "trapped in the exhausting embrace of his father's altruism." Thinking of his recent military service, he again feels discouraged. "If he had not done any actual combat, that had not been his fault. He had been there, but no one had called on him." The opening chapter ends with Anthony, ready to leave for Saint Mansard, brooding alone: "For one great and blinding moment, Anthony thought of striking out after his father and revolting. The moment, however, quickly passed, and Anthony compromised by feeling extremely sorry for himself." After this opening chapter, the tone of the story shifts completely as this realistic father-son conflict scene is followed by a superficial adventure story with some satiric elements.

Saint Mansard is, and isn't, Notre Dame. O'Connor's fictitious college in this story is a non-sectarian school without any clergymen around, but its central architectural feature is "a big gold overcoat on the steeple" (the "Golden Dome" is Notre Dame's symbolic center); it has a reputation for its bone-crushing athletic teams; it was founded in the early 1800's in a log cabin (as was Notre Dame); and it is located on the outskirts of Fender, Indiana (the Studebaker auto plant used to be South Bend's largest industry). The institution has had a varied history as a grammar school, an Indian school, a Jesuit college until the Ku Klux Klan burned it, and an agricultural institute. It was ready for oblivion when it was suddenly rescued by federal funds poured into it during the war for the use of the college as a training facility.

Some of these facts parallel Notre Dame history closely enough so that it is reasonable to say that O'Connor was writing a mild satire about his *alma mater.*

The satiric elements cluster around the problems of a chaotic curriculum, apathetic students, and the cynical advice given by fellow faculty members to the idealistic new teacher, Anthony Cantwell. For example, Anthony is supposed to teach a course in Balkan religious history, a subject he knows nothing about; his students are dull except for one eager, brilliant ex-seminarian. (A few years later, Kingsley Amis' *Lucky Jim* would have the same basic situation: Jim vs. Mitchie.) A fellow teacher, "Ripper" Dyer, advises Anthony that, if this student gives him any trouble in class, Anthony should "hint that he was unfrocked for moral reasons." But such humor in the story functions as an incidental background setting, for it is overshadowed by a complicated and melodramatic "intrigue" plot.

On his arrival at Saint Mansard, Anthony meets Wallace William Horse, an eccentric old faculty member, and "Ripper" Dyer, a young teacher, irresponsible but amiable, the iconoclastic "pal" of students. Afterwards, Anthony meets Dean Aram Juliet, an exotic expatriate whose office has secret doors and who has rigged the campus with hidden microphones and peepholes. Dean Juliet is ready to reject Anthony's teaching credentials as being insufficient when he notes that Senator Mayhew, the friend of Anthony's father, has recommended him. Later, in the cafeteria, Anthony meets the beautiful Carol Frain, daughter of the ex-dean, and Gideon McCoy, an exposé journalist. McCoy wants to enlist Anthony to spy on the activities of Dean Juliet because McCoy is gathering evidence of a "secret conspiracy" by the dean and Senator Mayhew to create federal control of education. "Ripper" Dyer is revealed as another undercover journalist investigating the dean. Anthony, attracted by Carol, agrees to help the cause. After lunch, he goes to the gymnasium where he meets an interesting minor character, Colonel "Beak" Burnside, who is the physical fitness director. "Beak," a health fanatic, is a tough old war hero; and he is fanatical not only about physical conditioning but about germicidal sprays. (This character reappears as General Walter "Beak" Blackburn in *The Oracle*, and, to a lesser extent, is suggestive of Charlie Hennessey in *The Last Hurrah*.) Following this meeting, Anthony meets Carol's father, a dignified contemplative man. The existing manuscript ends at this point, in mid-sentence at the bottom of the page; there is no way of telling how much more O'Connor wrote of this story.

IV Free-Lancing: the Unpublished Manuscripts

O'Connor stayed in Boston after he was discharged from the service at the end of the war. For a year he returned to radio, working at WNAC as a writer-announcer with the Yankee network. Then, deciding to concentrate on his own writing, he quit his job in October, 1946, and began the precarious existence of a free-lance writer, determined to support himself and to write "the novel." During the next decade, he lived frugally and on the borderline of poverty in furnished rented rooms. Enamored with Boston, O'Connor always stayed close to the heart of the city; his various rooming houses were never more than a few steps away from Boston Common, and he spent a good portion of every day walking or bicycling through the streets of the older part of the city adjacent to that park. In this period as a free-lance writer, he worked on a prolific number of odd jobs (journalism, editing, teaching writing for a year at Boston College's night school, etc.) and on assorted personal writings, many of these things being done simultaneously. Thus, an exact chronological order of his work is impossible, but his writings can be roughly grouped for discussion in the convenient categories of "unpublished" and "published" work of this period.

Unpublished manuscripts, written when he lived at 426 Beacon Street or 194 Beacon Street (1946), include three satiric sketches. "Something Has Died Within Me, Sirs!" (8 pp.) is a humorous piece about the narrator's resignation from the Book of the Month Club, written as if it were an *exclusive* club. The narrator recollects the good old days when he used to sprawl over the leather chairs in the oak-panelled rooms of the club enjoying the cozy fellowship of fellow *literati*. In "The Interview" (8 pp.) a reporter comes to interview a coast guardsman, recently returned from Greenland, who is a talkative, rambling storyteller; the frustrated interviewer's questions are never answered as the sailor keeps going off on irrelevant sidetracks. *"As It Was in the Beginning"* (6 pp.) is a re-write of parts of the second chapter of the "Coast Guard" manuscript; it is the story of Boyd Lorenzo, the young "con" man whom O'Connor met in Florida, who profits by gulling strong, dumb soldiers into his "stable" of semi-professional wrestlers.

Unpublished short story manuscripts, written while O'Connor was at 5 Brimmer Street (1947–48), include "Here She is, in Person!" (7 pp.), a set of vignettes about the decline of vaudeville with brief sketches of an awkward ballerina, a pretentious harmonica player, a lecherous fat comedian, and an aging movie queen. "The Coward" (14 pp.) is a contrived, melodramatic story about a forty-one-year-old "failure" who attempts to be a hero to his son. The man, scorned by his wife and his law office associates, seeks the boy's admiration; during a day's outing, the father's pretense of bravery is almost shaken several times and is finally destroyed when a bullying stranger humiliates him by forcing him to apologize for an accident he didn't cause. "Family Man" (18 pp.) has a young narrator, who is traveling through Indiana on the train, meet a garrulous journalist, a bubbling optimist who sees the best in even the worst scoundrel. The journalist introduces the narrator to a notorious mobster whose "human interest" story comes out as he tells how he has adopted six children—not because of any lack of sexual potency on his part, but because of an odd eugenic idea of "good breeding": to avoid the risks of hereditary or birth malformations, the mobster prefers to select his children from the well-formed, intelligent babies at an orphanage in an exclusive suburb.

During this period, O'Connor made another attempt at writing a novel. The "Luther Sudworth" manuscript is an untitled fragment (43 pp.) of a spoof novelette about an ignorant country bumpkin, Luther Sudworth, who leaves Maine to find a job in New York City. Luther applies at a radio broadcasting network station where he is immediately hired as a commentator because of his suitable background and his intelligence for this position. Promoted to vice-president, Luther becomes the arbiter of taste for programming. Several types of radio programs (interview shows, advice counselors, etc.) are satirized in subsequent scenes, but the level of writing does not rise above a third-rate imitation of Max Schulman.

In 1949, O'Connor moved to 11 Marlborough Street, just across the street from the *Atlantic*'s office. During the next seven years here, he wrote *The Oracle* and most of *The Last Hurrah*. Of the four unpublished manuscripts written here, one seems to have been written fairly early or about 1949. "The Breathing Meter" (6 pp.) is a whimsical fantasy about a tax commissioner who gets the idea of taxing "the very air we breathe." He gets legislation passed to require metered masks for all of the state's citizens and then hires an advertising agency to promote the campaign: "breathing fresh air is communistic, because Joe Stalin had been breathing fresh air all of his life." Corrupt meter-fixers and fresh-air bootleggers flourish under the new law, and several thrifty old New Englanders die by trying to economize on breathing.

Another story, "The Greatest Salesman in Rhode Island (Potentially)" (12 pp.) can be dated in 1950; its main character is related in spirit to Christopher Usher, the protagonist of *The Oracle*, which was also written that year. This brief story is an autobiographical account of O'Connor's first job in radio. He relates the zealous pep talk given by the enthusiastic station manager to convince him, a new announcer, of the sacredness of his calling; at the end of the story, the disillusioned narrator overhears the same speech being given to his replacement. An earlier draft of this same story begins with O'Connor's own feelings of inadequacy during his first job-hunting experience: "Ten years ago, fresh from college, and with the special lack of professional aptitude that marks the authentic A.B., it was my good fortune to enter the magic world of radio."

The other two unpublished stories in this period relate directly to *The Last Hurrah*: "C.B." (18 pp.) concerns a garrulous old man, Cornelius Bernard Cullinan, who is obsessed with health fads and medical gadgets and who visits the hospitals every week "to keep up with Science." The story revolves around his idea of using a Polaroid camera to record the daily changes in the appearances of hospital patients. O'Connor repeated this anecdote with Charlie Hennessey in *The Last Hurrah* and, later, with "Doctor" Billy Ryan in *I Was Dancing*. An editor called this repetition to his attention, but O'Connor was delighted with the anecdote and saw no reason not to repeat the joke. In "De Mortuis" (18 pp.), the young narrator visits his Uncle Martin, a small town politician, who invites the youth to go with him to Knocko Minihan's wake— a scene, slightly revised, that is incorporated in *The Last Hurrah*. The politician-uncle, seeking votes at the wake, leaves the observer-nephew in the hands of the old crone Delia Boylan, who points out the Carmichael girls, Johnny the undertaker, and others. For the novel, O'Connor filled out the scene (adding the kitchen incident, etc.) and made appropriate revisions in the characterization of the uncle.

V *Free-lancing: the Published Writings*

Not all of O'Connor's apprentice work was rejected; he did manage to publish enough to eke out a living and to keep his hopes alive. One source of income and satisfaction was his "Roger Swift" column in the *Boston Herald*. Three times a week, for fifteen dollars a column, O'Connor wrote under this pseudonym a column in which he reviewed current radio and television programs. However, these essays were not the mainstay of his ambition in writing; more likely he was concerned with the professional editorial reactions of the *Atlantic* staff than with the popular reception of his journalism.

Shortly after O'Connor settled in Boston, he began a most extraordinary relationship with the *Atlantic* staff. Almost daily, for the next twenty-two years, O'Connor was a welcome visitor in their offices on Arlington Street; for he stopped there, almost daily, to share a coffee break or lunch with the various editors and staff members. He became a permanent, unofficial, member of the *Atlantic* family, in an association of mutual respect and affection. It was a friendship which could tolerate adverse conditions; the *Atlantic*, for example, rejected O'Connor's first novel manuscript and many stories and articles which he submitted, but these professional decisions did not alter the relationship. O'Connor respected the expertise of the *Atlantic* staff, and they, in turn, respected his ability and promise as a writer.

The friendship was not a solemn one. O'Connor was a delightful, personable, buoyant visitor who entered the office with a joke, a soft-shoe dance, an imitation of some local character, or a magic trick he had just learned. For both O'Connor and the *Atlantic* staff, these visits were welcome breaks from the tensions of work; for O'Connor's own daily writing habits were rather fixed. He rose very early in the morning, write for four or five hours, then took his break with the *Atlantic* staff. Afterwards, he frequently spent the afternoons walking through the streets of Boston talking to the many friends and acquaintances he encountered. Usually in the evenings he sketched notes for the next morning's work. As he followed this alternating pattern, from silent isolation to gregarious camaraderie, O'Connor was careful and considerate not to impinge upon or to interrupt the working periods of his friends; the daily breaks were well timed for the mutual benefit of all.

The first literary results of O'Connor's association with the *Atlantic* appeared as a series of four light essays satirizing contemporary radio programs. These articles, in the "Accent on Living" section, indicated O'Connor's wit, his familiarity with radio, his rejection of the vulgar and the meretricious, his concern with structural patterns, and his satiric insight. Although dated today because they deal with ephemeral matters, they legitimately deserved publication in the entertainment section. "The Fairly Merry Widow" (June, 1946) described the daily soap-operas, especially the ubiquitous "widow" programs, such as "Valiant Lady," "Ma Perkins," "Road of Life," and "Portia Faces Life." The second essay, "No Laughing Matter" (September, 1946), analyzed the structural format of the comedy programs: "they all subscribe faithfully to the same blueprint, an architectural pattern." Here, O'Connor pointed out the stock elements in the programs of Eddie Cantor, Bob Hope, and Rudy Vallee ("Rudy's program interests me only because I suspect that it is being written by my dentist.") But this otherwise satiric essay is concluded with a serious praise of Fred Allen whom O'Connor sees as the "spiritual affiliate of Ring Lardner and Peter Finley Dunne" and as radio's first satirist of adult proportions, a man with a civilized mind and an unequaled sense of comedy.

In the third essay, "Here in the Studio . . ." (October, 1946), O'Connor analyzed the switch in emphasis as radio shows began to gear their programs to entertain *studio* audiences rather than to the unseen listening public. Programs such as "Truth or Consequences," "People Are Funny," and "Queen for a Day" could be fully understood only by the studio witnesses; and their inexplicable laughter in reaction to sight gags, stunts, gestures, and expressions was broadcast to a baffled listening audience. O'Connor then fantasized what would happen if this practice spread to Broadway where plays would be put on behind the drawn curtain and a knowledgeable announcer would tell the assembled audience what was going on behind it. In the fourth piece, "Prove You're Human" (February, 1947), O'Connor changed to a dramatic presentation, a parody of the inane dialogue between the master of ceremonies of a quiz program and a typical contestant; O'Connor's mimicry of the language patterns and mental attitudes of these people is well done.

Later that year, a short story, "The Gentle Perfect Knight," (September, 1947), was published as an *Atlantic* "First." O'Connor was delighted; in his reply to editor Edward Weeks' acceptance of the story, O'Connor wrote: "Your letter was one of the first that I have received from an editorial office that was not a cheerful mimeograph reminding me of the historic example of Robert Bruce and his silly spider." O'Connor's first published piece of fiction centers on a twenty-seven-year-old, unmarried girl who is known as "poor" Iris by her zealous matchmaking married friends. Invited to dinner to meet Camilla's bachelor cousin, who has just returned from an Arctic exploration trip, Iris is prepared to meet a dud. Surprisingly, the explorer is young and handsome; Iris begins thinking that she has met her gentle, perfect knight. But, as the meal and the conversation continue, the young man reveals himself to be a "vulgar monomaniac" absorbed in the subject of eating pemmican and raw meat. As he details his barbaric culinary adventures, Iris is disillusioned and sickened.

O'Connor's second story in the *Atlantic*, "The Inner Self" (April, 1950), appeared three years later; and the introduction mentions that he is dividing his time between his first novel and his short stories and satires. In this story, a thirty-year-old widow, dreamy and withdrawn, is at a cocktail party at her sister-in-law's house. The young widow remains aloof from the guests, knowing that none can meet her high standards for friendship. An older man introduces himself as *Doctor* Bernard Brady and ingratiates himself by making condescending remarks about the other guests and by noting that she alone is *simpático*. As he relates the boring history of his moustache, she begins to envision herself as his accomplice in science; his homely face begins to assume a rugged Lincolnesque quality. She first deduces that he is a surgeon; later she assumes him to be a psychiatrist. The spell is broken when the sister-in-law stops by and speaks about him as "Bernie, the dentist." Disillusioned, with "a man who spent his days poking about in other people's mouths," the widow returns to her original fantasies of seeking a perfect friendship.

Both stories seem derivative from Joyce's "Araby," the disillusionment of the naive dreamer. Of interest here is that some of the problems of loneliness and the search for a "perfect friend" that an idealistic young *bachelor* might face are dramatized by female characters whose ages correspond to that of O'Connor when he is writing these stories. If O'Connor is projecting some of his own inner anxieties in these stories, the significant thing is his awareness of the folly of the characters; the dreamy girls are presented with sympathy, but the writer is detached and gently amused by their naive idealism.

"Parish Reunion," published in *The Yale Review* of September, 1950 (59–69), is O'Connor's only appearance in the academic-literary journals. A well-written story, with tight economical style, it seems to have been influenced by J. F. Powers' scenes of clerical life in *Prince of Darkness* (1947). Some of the minor characters and situations of *The Edge of Sadness* can be recognized, or are foreshadowed, in the crazy janitor and the gregarious back-slapping priest in "Parish Reunion." The story takes place at the annual parish reunion of Saint Brendan's, an event which has grown so popular that it has been moved to the ballroom of a downtown hotel. Father Desmond Sugrue, the pastor, is a man of such aloof dignity that his parishioners suspect that he is an Anglican. He regards this reunion as a dubious activity, a "noisy, purposeless jamboree," which he has to endure because of the enthusiastic insistence of his curate, Father Karski, "a man of inexhaustible energy and ideas; from him poured a ceaseless, bewildering stream of plans for lawn parties, barbecues, smokers, bridges, beanoes, and monster outdoor rallies." At the reunion, the pastor notices the gregarious Father Karski demonstrating his golf stances and techniques to a crowd of onlookers; the pastor remembers that Father Karski had once asked him "if there was anything in canon law to prevent a priest's becoming the Amateur Golfing Champion of the United States."

After being trapped in conversation with a pious, old, complaining woman and an obsequious contractor, the pastor sees Looney Noonan, the parish janitor, a humble man who enjoys long periods of sanity between mild fits when he imagines himself a priest. Looney begins to put on a pantomime, wearing a priest's biretta, walking around with a pompous strutting gait, smiling, shaking hands, and making gestures of an exaggerated camaraderie. When he captures the attention of the whole crowd, Looney starts an elaborate pantomime of playing golf. Only then does the pastor understand the gist of the parody, and looking at the vain Father Karski's reddened face, the pastor realizes that he, too, has comprehended the reason for the crowd's laughter. Slyly the pastor gloats, "rolling over in his imagination the conversations which would take place in the rectory preceding next year's parish reunion."

While O'Connor was completing *The Oracle*, several ephemeral pieces in the *Atlantic* kept the pot boiling at home. "What Night Does to Baseball" (August, 1950) is an exposition of the advantages (profit to the owners) and the disadvantages (trouble to the players and the game) of the growth of scheduling night baseball games. "It's Spontaneous" (January, 1951) praises a local radio station's quiz program as being an intelligent exception to the usual idiotic quiz shows of the time. "Words Without Music" (November, 1951) traces the development of the disc jockey from his former role as anonymous announcer to that of the loud-mouthed "personality."

After *The Oracle* was published, during the years in which O'Connor was writing *The Last Hurrah*, five brief articles appeared in the *Atlantic*. "Halls of Ivy" (November, 1952) is a light fantasy about a student who is preparing for graduation from a professional disc jockey school. "The Case of the Sober Shamus" (June, 1953) laments the plight of the television detective, a sober dud, who is unable to take a drink on duty. "Gold Among the Boo-Hoos" (February, 1954) satirizes television programs, such as "Strike It Rich," which use human misery and catastrophe to lure viewers to witness grief-stricken contestants vying for money and prizes. "The Meet at Cabinteely" (July, 1954) is a travel piece that resulted from O'Connor's visit to Ireland, and it reports an informal horse race in rural Ireland, an atmosphere of country people and simple pleasures. "The Indirect Approach" (June, 1955) considers the off-beat television commercials in which the sponsor's message follows after a scene seemingly unrelated to the product advertised.

In this era, Edward Weeks, the editor of the *Atlantic*, also broadcasted a weekly national radio program, "Writers of Today." Although Weeks was an experienced speaker, he thought that O'Connor's radio experience would be helpful in the preparation

of this network series. For over two years (1948–49), Weeks hired
O'Connor at fifty dollars a week to listen to his rehearsal and to
criticize his delivery. Weeks was thus able to provide partial living expenses for the struggling young writer in a way in which
O'Connor could legitimately perform a useful service. A few years
later, when O'Connor was working on *The Last Hurrah*, Weeks
again came to his aid with another special project, one most welcomed by O'Connor. For several years, Weeks had been trying
to persuade Fred Allen to edit a collection of Allen's radio scripts.
Allen, who had always felt that he was too busy, finally consented
to Weeks' plan.

Weeks invited O'Connor to New York to meet Allen. O'Connor
had long been an admirer of Allen's ability and, at this meeting,
Allen was immediately delighted with O'Connor. (A close friendship later developed; O'Connor's second trip to Ireland, in 1954,
was with Fred Allen and his wife.) Returning to Boston with
thirty large volumes of Allen's radio scripts, O'Connor began the
reading, selecting, and editing of the scripts which comprised
Allen's book *Treadmill to Oblivion* (1954). O'Connor, a constant
listener of the Allen show, was able to cull through the mass of
material efficiently and to select representative segments so that
Allen could write the continuity interludes. The success of this
collection encouraged Allen to write his autobiography, *Much
Ado About Me* (1956). Allen died before he finished this book,
but the almost-completed manuscript was published with an
"Epilogue" by O'Connor explaining his part in the composition
process of the book.

One result of O'Connor's visit to Ireland was a critique of British television, "Do They Want It Dull?" which was published in
Life on November 2, 1953 (109–16). After describing the third-
rate, music-hall vaudeville shows, the fifth-rate comedians, the
static non-news news broadcasts, and the omnipresent health programs nagging about "man's decay and mortality," O'Connor
concluded that the BBC may not be vulgar, but it was certainly
dull and boring. Fred Allen, in a letter to O'Connor, praised the
humor of this article: "more entertainment in your piece than
there is in the whole bloody medium as it is operated under the
BBC setup."

After *The Last Hurrah* was published, the economic pressure
was alleviated, and O'Connor was able to concentrate on his

fiction. For convenience, the few minor publications after 1956 are mentioned in this chapter, out of chronological order, because he did so little writing other than the novels. His only short story, in the *Atlantic* (October, 1957), was "A Grand Day for Mr. Garvey," a story which is closely related to—and possibly the genesis of—his novel, *I Was Dancing*. In this short story, old Mr. Garvey has been humiliated by being sent to a rest home by his niece and her husband. Although the old man finds the home very congenial, each week he plays The Game with his visiting niece: feigning unhappiness, he tries to make her feel guilty about her "cruel" decision. His subtle, calculated complaints are deftly parried by the cheerful counterpunches of the young niece whose skill at The Game almost matches his.

Five years after Skeffington's debut, O'Connor related the aftermath of that publication in an *Atlantic* article of September, 1961, "James Michael Curley and *The Last Hurrah*," which tells of Mayor Curley's identification with Skeffington and of O'Connor's constant denials. "For Whom the Novelist Writes," in *The Critic* (April-May, 1963, 13–17), is the text of the speech delivered at the Thomas More Association when O'Connor received an award from that Catholic literary group for *The Edge of Sadness*. This article reflects O'Connor's thinking about his own position as one who has achieved a wide popular audience but has been denied an enthusiastic response from the critics. In December, 1964, an *Atlantic* "Bonus" published the opening section of O'Connor's novel-in-progress (*All in the Family*) under the title of "One Spring Morning." The brief review of *Michael Field's Cooking School* cookbook, in *Life* (July 16, 1965, p. 21), is atypical of O'Connor's avoidance of review writing in his later years, but the explanation lies in O'Connor's own enthusiasm as an amateur chef and in his friendship with Michael Field. O'Connor's last appearance in the *Atlantic* was as a "guest contributor," substituting for his sick friend, Charles Morton. In this essay, "The Book Fair" (July, 1966), O'Connor humorously describes three of these "curious entertainments where a handful of writers may talk on the congenial subject of themselves."

Although O'Connor's own writing in the *Atlantic* diminished, his close relationship with the magazine continued. The first important critique by a major literary historian, Howard Mumford Jones, appeared in "Politics, Mr. O'Connor, and the Family

Novel" (October, 1966), an essay analyzing *All in the Family* in terms of O'Connor's total achievement as an "heir" of the "great tradition" of the novel. Two years later, the *Atlantic* (May, 1968) phrased O'Connor's special obituary notice as "a death in the family" and noted the intensity of the mutual friendship. In July, 1968, the *Atlantic* published a memoir by Professor John V. Kelleher, "Edwin O'Connor and the Irish-American Process," which not only related personal anecdotes but also evaluated some of O'Connor's literary contributions. In the following year, Edmund Wilson contributed "The Great Baldini: A Memoir and a Collaboration" (November, 1969), in which the fragment of a proposed novel by O'Connor and Wilson appeared, together with Wilson's commentary on O'Connor as a man and as a writer. In 1970, *The Best and the Last of Edwin O'Connor* was published by Atlantic-Little, Brown; on is jacket was the succinct tribute: "As publishers, we hope we have done him justice. He was our pride as an author and our joy as a friend."

CHAPTER 3

The Oracle

I *Background*

DRAWING from his knowledge and experience as a radio announcer for two years and, later, as a radio critic, Edwin O'Connor's first novel, *The Oracle* (1951), was about a nationally prominent radio commentator, the oracle of the network, Christopher Usher. Christopher ("Christ-Bearer") is a self-appointed messiah, for he seriously believes in his own mission. Although everyone who knows Christopher personally is aware of his failings, only Christopher and his loyal (and remote) audience of five million retain an idealized version. Schlesinger's "Introduction" (to *The Best and the Last of Edwin O'Connor*) summarized the story as "two weeks of crisis when Usher attempts to outmaneuver his sponsor and improve his contract; and it dealt lovingly with his microphone manner (nauseating), his politics (reactionary), his sex life (active but unspecific) and his vanity (bottomless)."

In several ways the book is dated, fixed firmly in its post-war *milieu*. Some of the topical allusions, loaded with satiric intent, are apt to be overlooked by the reader today who is unaware of the connotations of some of the offhand remarks by the characters. Christopher, for example, plans to call Louis Budenz (the ex-Communist, darling of right-wing columnists) for an "authoritative" analysis of Soviet public opinion; and there are many allusions to contemporary politics ("Mao Tse-Tung and his Muscovite masters," Edouard Benes, Jan Masaryk, Tom Dewey, Jim Farley, Eleanor Roosevelt, Homer Capehart, UNESCO, etc.) which demand a knowledgeable audience. But even more important is the decline in status of radio as a *serious* medium of communication. A later generation could hardly imagine the importance of radio, and of the radio commentator, in the pre-television era; nor would a younger generation (which is accustomed to the

bland neutrality of television newscasting) have a full appreciation of the blatant ideological slant of the radio news commentators of the 1940's and 1950's, a variety of Americana now de-
funct.

Schlesinger (p. 6) noted that *The Oracle* was "inspired by
Gabriel Heatter and Cedric Foster, broadcasters of the late forties
whose orotund pomposities delighted Ed and stimulated him to
marvelous mimicry. It also drew on a flatulent Boston newspaper
columnist named Bill Cunningham." If one balks at the credibility
of Christopher Usher's optimism or egocentricity, it would be well
to read Gabriel Heatter's autobiography, *There's Good News
Tonight* (1960).

The Oracle was first conceived of as a three-act play; but, after
some preliminary stage sketches and a partial draft, O'Connor
discarded this plan and wrote the story in the form of a novel.
He submitted the manuscript, originally entitled *Top of the
World,* to the Atlantic Monthly Press in early 1950. By this time,
he had been writing for the *Atlantic* sporadically during the previous four years and had established a warm personal friendship
with the editorial staff. Yet, the manuscript was turned down,
after seven readings, and the book was eventually published by
Harpers. Despite this rejection, O'Connor's relationship with the
Atlantic remained unbroken; and the next manucript (*The Last
Hurrah*) that he submitted won the Atlantic Prize and subsequently became one of the most commercially successful books
ever published by that long-established house.

II   *The Novel*

The Oracle begins with Christopher Usher standing naked,
sweating in the sweltering heat of a closed studio, broadcasting
his daily radio news commentary to his five million faithful listeners. Although his nudity could be rationally explained and
justified by the almost unendurable heat of the summer day,
Christopher is vaguely aware of the sensual overtones of his unseen exhibitionism. Thus, immediately in the opening scene (reprinted in *The Best and the Last of Edwin O'Connor,* 41–47),
three major themes are established that are continued throughout
the book: Christopher's public unctuousness, his private sensu-

ality, and the listening audience's ignorance of the private man behind the public façade.

After the broadcast, Christopher joins his wife, Meredith, at a cocktail party in a scene which not only serves to introduce his wife and his father-in-law, Dr. Edmund Wrenn, but also shows Christopher in action at the party as he seeks the center of attention, domineers his acquaintances, and plays the game of one-upmanship. His need for an attentive, believing audience is counterpointed by the reactions of those who know him best. Christopher has a lingering doubt that his wife has a "small, alien spring of irreverence" in her, and the slightest hint of her inattention or incredulity is taken by him as an almost-treasonable mockery of him. But there is no doubt about the antagonism of his father-in-law, Dr. Wrenn, who does not conceal his distaste for Christopher. Dr. Wrenn is the first appearance of a familiar O'Connor character—the embittered, incisive cynic. He continually goads his son-in-law by talking about Christopher's earlier career as a sports reporter, a less-glorious role than his present exalted position, and a topic which Christopher prefers to ignore. When Christopher is involved with others at the party, Dr. Wrenn is even less subtle about his feelings as he speaks in private to his daughter.

Leaving the party, Christopher meets his mistress, Lura Andriescu. Here the lurid stereotype of the kept woman is consciously exaggerated for humor: Lura (born Etta Pendergast) waits for her lover-man in a secret love-nest (known about by winking elevator boys) which is decorated in the style of a low-budget Hollywood movie. Zebra wallpaper, a large plastic fireplace with imitation glowing coals, an artificial polar bear rug, and a voluptuous divan provide the setting for the introduction to this woman of "pneumatic luxuriance" who is munching bon-bons while wriggling in her satin dress. O'Connor's parody of the stereotype may be a bit heavy-handed, but it is humorous, and it certainly is not the unintentional mistake of an amateur.

The second chapter focuses primarily on Christopher's daily routine as he works at the broadcasting studio. Christopher's opening of the morning's mail gives O'Connor an opportunity to exhibit his wit about letter writing from different *personae:* from enthusiastic admirers, from a club-program chairman seeking a cut-rate on a lecture fee, from a paranoiac claiming treasonable conspiracy in government circles, and from semi-literate "plain folks" of the Bible Belt. After the mail, the reading of magazines is Christopher Usher's next duty; and the diverse selection of titles indicates the dominant interests and the superficiality of this self-appointed expert on everything. A visit from Mr. Churchill Chan, a propagandist for the Chiang Kai-shek government, completes the morning's information gathering. When Chan seeks to encourage Christopher to plead for American military support to China, Christopher, an ardent anti-Communist, differs with Chan about the method for saving China. In Christopher's uncomplicated view, the major problem is to uplift the spiritual energies of the Chinese people. To rouse them from their apathy, Christopher is convinced that *his* idea of delivering inspirational comic books, via low-level American airplanes flying over the peasants' fields, is the only solution. Chan craftily tries to persuade Christopher of the advantage and economy of both leaflets *and* bombs being carried by the planes. The wit duel here (reprinted in *The Best and the Last of Edwin O'Connor,* 47–51), is an excellent piece of humorous writing.

As the first chapter introduces the conflict in Christopher's domestic life, the function of the second chapter is to introduce the conflict in his business life. After preparing for his daily broadcast, Christopher goes to the office of Adam Flair, the vice president of the radio network, to inform him that he is planning to ask for a large increase in salary from his sponsor; and at this point the novel begins to fall into what would soon become a common pattern in novels written about the radio and television industry. *The Oracle* is one of the first of a rash of novels that detail the executive backstabbing in the communications business; Adam Flair can be recognized as an early appearance of a now-familiar stereotype (apparently with some basis in fact) of the baby-faced hatchetman, the smiling cobra, the jaded cynical manipulator whose business mask is that of the young alert executive. Opposed to Christopher's plan to seek a raise, Adam warns of the possible disaster if Christopher overplays his hand and tries to force an unreasonable price for his services. When Christopher leaves the room, Adam's comments to a secretary reveal his antipathy to Christopher. Later, Christopher, while taking his accustomed afternoon nap, dreams; and, in a montage of pleasant scenes, he sees himself associating with popes and presidents and sailing in a tropical sea with his nubile Lura. In high optimism, he awakes to deliver his broadcast.

The next day, General Walter Blackburn, an old friend, arrives for an extended visit at the house of Usher. The old general, like Christopher, is a self-deluded man. Bursting with optimism to cover his repressed disappointment, the general sees himself as being unjustly treated by those in command who have assigned him the job of inspecting historic forts in order to keep him out of Washington. The general, like Christopher, tends to over-simplify everything: for him, "the so-called H-Bomb" is just another weapon. General Blackburn lives in a world of reminiscences of the good old days, of Spads and Fokkers and Caproni triplanes, of Verdun and Black Jack Pershing and the Rose of No Man's Land. While staying at Christopher's house, the general receives a new assignment to lecture at the local high schools "where, under the wild misapprehension that the youths seated sullenly before him aspired to immediate enlistment, he spoke in glowing terms of the military life" and illustrated his speeches with personal adventures of early morning rising, healthy cold baths, and long marches in the nippy air. At first, the general is a welcomed household guest as he and Christopher talk to each other for hours, each on a different subject, and both totally absorbed in their own monologues. Later, the general's talking begins to annoy Christopher who prefers someone to listen to him. General Blackburn's functional role in the novel is minor, he acts as the unwitting catalyst to precipitate the domestic crisis, but his characterization is evidence of O'Connor's early interest and skill in developing this type of garrulous old man.

In the meantime, Christopher attends the crucial meeting with the sponsor of his radio program, Bernie Udolpho, a crude self-made millionaire who has gained his fortune by his shrewd business acumen in peddling various salves and lotions. Adam Flair and the other network executives who attend the meeting expect that Christopher will be outmanuevered—and probably fired—by the wily Udolpho. Christopher, gambling on his own usefulness to Udolpho's purpose, is ready to ask for the increase in salary. After some preliminary verbal rites, and a monologue by Udolpho about his European trip, which emphasize what a gross commercialist he is, Christopher makes his move and delivers his sales pitch. Complete with facts and figures that document his popularity, the size of his audiences and their devotion to him, Christopher confidently states his case as a sound business proposition, profitable to them both. Udolpho listens, enigmatically, then tells Christopher that he'll think about it.

Christopher senses that he has won his victory, and he is jubilant the next day as he prepares to leave on a ten-day lecture tour in the Midwest. The emphasis in this scene of the lecture tour (reprinted in *The Best and the Last of Edwin O'Connor,* 51–55) focuses on the rhetorical strategy of the "seasoned campaigner" preparing for his speech. With a keen insight into the audience's mentality, Christopher needs but a few facts of local information—"leading citizen. . . . imp. histor. events . . . princ. lodges, societies . . . items local humor"—in order to adapt his all-purpose speech, "One World and Your World," to any of the small towns he visits. The speech itself caters to the prejudices and preconceptions of the rural audience by favorably comparing the goodness of rural America to the wicked ways of Washington and the rest of the world: "the world came off rather badly. On one hand there was disorder, poverty, impiety, a polyglot chaos; on the other hand, there was neatness, abundance, faith, a resolved monolingual blend. On the one hand was the way of Ev Mosper, the Casper Stanwell Post, The Hero of Tippecanoe; on the other, the way of Stalin, Mao, the State Department, the crafty British, the venal French." O'Connor's interest in the skill and the craftsmanship of the professional manipulator of words is a foreshadowing of his fuller treatment of this theme in *The Last Hurrah* in which Frank Skeffington's strategies and techniques in capturing an audience are given great attention. Christopher Usher, like Frank Skeffington, is fluent and voluble, dextrous and nimble in adjusting to the mood of an audience, all with a seemingly natural, effortless ease.

While Christopher is on the lecture tour, he continues his regular radio program, broadcasting from the various local network affiliates. One such broadcast is used by O'Connor as a device for plot continuity to show the reactions of the various characters to Christopher's words: Adam Flair responds with cynical comments, Meredith Usher listens silently, General Blackburn gives enthusiastic vocal support, Chan's co-workers hear about the China scheme in stunned disbelief, Bernie Udolpho meditates on

Christopher's utility to him, and Lura Andriescu, faithless to her lover, tunes in a Hollywood gossip program.

On Christopher's return from the lecture tour, he stops overnight in Washington where he attends a party. This party scene serves primarily as a vehicle for satirical jabs at a variety of recognizable types: the brassy, vulgar, musical-comedy songstress who has been appointed as an ambassador (Perle Mesta?), the popular clergyman noted for his bland platitudes (Norman Vincent Peale?), the provincial Western senator, the party-line Russian attaché, and the exposé reporter with hints of conspiracy in the Vatican. O'Connor presents a hurried tour through a crowd of stereotypes until Christopher meets a gloomy advertising man named Keisler whose reputation is that of the Prophetic Messenger of bad, but accurate, news. Keisler, as the morose gossip who always has the inside information, is a caricature too; but he has a functional role since he implants the first hint of doom in Christopher's mind. After Keisler tells Christopher that he has heard the rumor, from an "excellent source," that Udolpho has decided to cancel Christopher's contract, Christopher begins to fear defeat for the first time since he has left the meeting with Udolpho. From this point in the novel, the tension continually builds as the repeated hints of disaster grow stronger.

When Christopher arrives in his home office, he meets with Adam Flair to discuss the negotiations with Udolpho. In this scene, there is the clearest presentation of "Cannibal politics," as television critic Edith Efron describes the internal workings of the networks; Efron (in *TV Guide*, January 10, 1970, 6) analyzing "network novels" from 1951 to 1969, notes: "Ego-pricking is the most popular indoor sport of the hierarchy, it appears from these novels. It is played all the way down the chain of command —everyone reveling in what an Edwin O'Connor VP gloatingly describes as 'the blunt, swift body blows to the self-esteem of a hireling.'" Adam Flair, exasperated with Christopher's pretentiousness and annoyed by the upset in routine caused by Christopher's personal involvement in the salary negotiations, delivers an ego-crushing tirade.

Christopher, infuriated, leaves the smiling Adam; but, once the initial rage passes, Christopher succumbs to fear and depression. Returning home, he seeks solace from Meredith, his long-suffering, understanding wife. His confidence revived by her,

Christopher plans to make his future broadcasts so good that he will definitely be indispensible. Yet, despite his best efforts (seen in fragmentary accounts of some of his grandiloquent broadcasts), a series of ominous incidents at the office plague him. Here, O'Connor draws from a long tradition of office humor about the executive whose job is in jeopardy. Little breaches of etiquette are now interpreted by Christopher as portents of doom: the janitor addresses him with a jaunty "Whaddaya say, Mac"; the barbershop in the building asks him to pay his bill promptly; Mr. Churchill Chan is seen ingratiating himself with a younger announcer; an unsigned poison-pen letter arrives, probably written by Adam Flair. In the meantime, the affair with Lura is beginning to disintegrate as she senses Christopher's precarious position. When Christopher accidently sees her on the street with another man, his fears increase as he recognizes that both his public and private lives are endangered. At a low ebb, he seeks religious consolation and visits a neighborhood Catholic Church, although he has never previously had an inclination for religious guidance.

At the church, he is met by an old priest, a stupid, pedantic man who has been interrupted while preparing his Sunday sermon which traces the liturgy of the Armenians, beginning with the Greek of St. Basil. Christopher's initial questions are answered with the priest's stock of moral platitudes, totally meaningless and irrelevant to the situation. Changing the tack, Christopher asks for religious literature "by some of your greatest people . . . some of your more advanced saints." The priest, thinking that he has met a kindred spirit, loads Christopher with stacks of dusty old volumes of Augustine, Aquinas, and St. John Chrysostom, all written in Latin. After Christopher leaves, the priest returns to his sermon manuscript: "He continued to write, happily and without hesitation. Each Sunday these sermons were attended to with enormous respect, having for his congregation all the fascination of the totally incomprehensible." This incident is not only another example of the self-deluded man, blissfully unaware of his own failings, but also an example of the brief vignettes of humorously grotesque characters who populate the fringe of O'Connor's world. Another such vignette appears earlier in the novel when Adam Flair mentions the career of the old actor who played the role of Sonny Muscle, the juvenile hero of a radio series: "The old man went to a surgeon; the result was that horrid teen-age squawk that stayed with him to the moment of his death. And he lived his role up to the hilt every minute of the day; as he became more senile, his identity became more deeply submerged in the personality of Sonny. In his last years he rarely talked of anything other than weenie roasts, juke boxes and hot rods."

On the night before the climactic day, when Christopher is to receive Udolpho's decision, Christopher and his wife quarrel. Christopher had been in the depths of self-pity, railing against the possible injustice that his great career, and the psyches of his five million faithful listeners, might be at the mercy of some gross commercialist. In this situation, Meredith's remark, that he had been "lucky" in his rise to fame, seems almost treasonable to Christopher. He leaves the house early the next morning, still pouting, and isolates himself in his office to await the expected telephone call from Udolpho. General Blackburn, who is still staying at the Usher house, plans to act as mediator in the family quarrel; he persuades Meredith that a reconciliation can be made more easily if the three of them go out that evening to a nightclub. When Meredith agrees, the general calls Christopher's office to tell him of their plan to meet him after the broadcast at the nightclub. The message, taken by a secretary, never reaches Christopher.

Christopher waits anxiously all day for the phone call from Udolpho. Fidgeting in the office, he begins to compose a script for the evening's broadcast which will be a nostalgic tour through his career as a commentator, a "simple, straightforward story of a man whose country owed him far more than it could ever hope to pay." When Udolpho's phone call does not come, Christopher delivers his broadcast, broods alone for a while afterwards, and returns home to an empty house. Depressed, he goes to Lura's apartment where he gets drunk very quickly and then recklessly suggests that they go to a nightclub together. As he enters the club with Lura, Christopher careens flat on the floor in front of Meredith and the general. This whole discovery episode and its climactic slapstick seem to be quite contrived and not subtle; the punch has been telegraphed to the reader the very moment that the general suggests the nightclub meeting. Nevertheless, this episode does serve the function of climaxing the sub-plot of Christopher's domestic conflict.

The morning after brings a hangover and remorse to Christopher, a farewell letter from the general, a cold reception from Meredith, and some melodramatic talk of divorce. When Christopher claims that Lura was a casual stranger, Dr. Wrenn reveals that he had known earlier, from a private detective, of Christopher's mistress and had told Meredith all about her. Defeated, Christopher goes to Lura's apartment where he finds her, bags packed, ready to leave with her former husband. Alone in his office again, Christopher sits despondently among his trophies, overwhelmed with pity for himself and his listeners. A phone call breaks the silence, and Christopher listens incredulously as Udolpho grunts out an approval for the increased salary. After a moment of shock, Christopher is euphoric with joy. The final lines show Christopher going to tell Adam Flair the good news. His is the triumph of the fool; still self-deluded, still unaware of what he is, self-satisfied and smug.

III *Critical Reaction*

The reviews of *The Oracle* were mixed. Probably the most pejorative review appeared in *Saturday Review* on May 26, 1951, (34) in which Nathan Rothman argued that the figure of the radio commentator was important enough in the society to deserve a full-scale assault but that *The Oracle* didn't deliver the blow because it was too much of a farce: "thin stuff, an approximation of all the popular jokes on commentators." Rothman's review provoked O'Connor's only public reply to a critic in *Saturday Review* ("Letters") on September 1, 1951; terming Rothman an unsatisfactory reporter, O'Connor noted two factual errors in the brief review.

The *Commonweal* review of July 27, 1951 (386) by Richard Wichert stated that the chief weakness of the book was in the predictable clichés of Usher's life, but he qualified this statement by observing that these are "perhaps inevitably imposed" by the subject matter. Describing the book as "biting comedy," Wichert observed that the "tragic fact is that the oracle *believes* what he says and, five million times worse, his listeners do too." The *Atlantic's* brief review of May, 1951 (79) was primarily a neutral précis; restrained, it ended with a polite compliment: "Like Saki, Mr. O'Connor has produced a caricature which comes outrageously close to reality." Al Capp's review, in the *New York Herald Tribune* of July 15, 1951 (6), praised the "hilarious account" of Christopher Usher and noted O'Connor's gift "for reproducing the idiot gabble of the worthlessly important." But Capp's real interest was in the "unwritten, but inescapably implied, story" which he thought was the serious core of the novel: "Underneath there is the other story, the story of American radio and its surrender to the beer-sellers and gadget vendors, by those into whose control the American people have given (for free) this priceless and powerful means of mass communication and influence—the networks."

Commercially, the book was a failure. O'Connor claimed that the American sales netted only seven hundred and twenty dollars, although the British sales were better, providing enough royalties to finance O'Connor's first trip to Ireland in 1953. The extent of O'Connor's disappointment with the reception of *The Oracle* may be deduced from several references he subsequently made about it; at least two times later, he repeated the story of this "disaster" and of a meeting with his publisher afterwards.

Twenty years later, Schlesinger's evaluation (pp.6–7) linked this novel to the influence of Evelyn Waugh, the British satirist who was popular at the time, especially in Catholic literary circles. Schlesinger commented: "Read today, *The Oracle* seems a satirical farce, influenced perhaps by the triumph of dunderheads in such books as *Scoop*. O'Connor was always a Waugh fan, and one feels here that he was trying for a Waugh tone. But the effects were a little broad. Christopher Usher was almost too smug and swinish; and, in general, the characters tended to dissolve into caricatures. . . . But the dialogue in *The Oracle* is mostly held in check. The novel evidently aimed to achieve English urbanity rather than Irish extravagance."

Although some topical allusions are dated, the reader today is apt to find *The Oracle* an enjoyable entertainment. It is not one of O'Connor's major works; but, if it is accepted for the light satire that it is, it can give delight as there is enough good writing in it to justify reading it for pleasure. However, if *The Oracle* is examined as a kind of rehearsal for O'Connor's later works, many of his characteristics and major themes can be found in this first published novel. His sense of structure is sound; he knows how to handle simultaneous sub-plots and how to weave the various elements together. O'Connor's humor, wit, satiric insight, and his ability to write a literate sentence are evident in *The Oracle,* although these qualities improve with the years. His keen ear for speech patterns, his gift of mimicry, and his love for the "comic grotesque" humorous character all appear, although, as Schlesinger noted, they are restrained. The extravagance and the exuberance of *The Last Hurrah* is not found in *The Oracle,* but many of the themes and characters foreshadow the second novel: O'Connor's interest in the *old* man, in the self-deluded man, in the cynic, in the professional manipulator of words and in the tricks of that trade. Finally, the most obvious link between this novel and *The Last Hurrah* is the triumph of the rogue at the end, a moral ambiguity which will be posed more seriously in *The Last Hurrah.*

CHAPTER 4

"A Young Man of Promise"

THE fictitious college in Indiana, this time called Mount Mansard, again serves as the setting for another attempted novel. This manuscript (227 pp.) which Schlesinger considered to be "a variation on the Enoch Arden theme," was written in 1950–51 after the publication of *The Oracle;* but O'Connor abandoned work on this manuscript when he suddenly started working on *The Last Hurrah,* incorporating some of the material from "A Young Man of Promise" into the novel about Skeffington. A knowledge of this unpublished manuscript is helpful in understanding part of the creative process involved in *The Last Hurrah,* in terms not only of the actual "borrowings" but also of the dynamics which motivate a writer.

The young man of promise in this story is the narrator, Kevin Rowan, who lives alone with his widowed father, the president of Mount Mansard College. Mount Mansard is a small, young college whose reputation has been built on "the spectacular brutality of its representatives on the playing field." The father had assumed the presidency nineteen years previously because of a good salary offer and the promise of academic reform. But such reform has not taken place: commencement exercises feature an anti-Communist speaker lecturing to a graduating class destined for careers in professional ball or as sporting-goods salesmen. The president is passively disappointed because the college hasn't "been reformed," and he spends his time quietly puttering around the library, reading, and keeping out of the way.

Kevin works as a cartoonist at the local newspaper, a job he holds because the newspaper's owner, old Amos Force, has a special liking for Kevin's comic strip "Little Simp." Some friction exists between Kevin and his father regarding this occupation; the father does not like his son's wasting his life on such a frivolous activity. But, other than that, Kevin, the narrator, says that their relationship is almost idyllic. Kevin summarizes his long years away from home, first at school and then in the service, and notes the new relationship established with his father after his return.

In the next chapter, Kevin goes to the newspaper office where the frugal-minded managing editor attempts to persuade him to become the contest editor. In this conversation, the "Boys Afloat" episode is related; and Burbank, the cynical journalist, enters. All of this material, with slight revisions, has been incorporated into *The Last Hurrah*.

Plot complication begins with the introduction of Uncle Timothy and Anna Archibald. Uncle Timothy, his father's brother, owns a chain of womens' specialty stores, but his real interest is in being a amateur theologian; he has a passion for nosing into the local diocesan affairs and for reporting to the bishop any breeches of "orthodoxy." This character appears, in revised form, as Roger Sugrue in *The Last Hurrah*. Anna Archibald, the love interest in the story, is the young, attractive "widow" of an undercover agent who has disappeared and who is presumed dead behind the Iron Curtain. She is introduced to Kevin by Uncle Timothy, who has been trying to convert her to Catholicism. Kevin's father, at the end of the chapter, points out the direction of the novel: "Now that is what I call an evening of diverison: a beautiful woman, a spy, a bit of practical theology. Rather like one of those entertaining books by your friend, Mr. Graham Greene. Had you thought of it in that light, I wonder?"

Back at the newspaper office, in the next chapter, Burbank is involved in reading the letters from the regular correspondents to his advice column (somewhat reminiscent of Nathanael West's *Miss Lonelyhearts*) while Kevin is involved in working out the "Argentina" episode of the Little Simp comic strip. Anna calls, asking Kevin to take care of a parking ticket for her because, as a foreigner, she doesn't know what to do with it. Kevin takes the ticket to be fixed by "Knocko" Noonan, a hanger-on at City Hall, who as a kid used to knock down doors with his head. Meeting Anna later, for lunch, Kevin tells her that Little Simp is a temporary sideline; ashamed of his job, he brags to her that he is writing a novel—"local setting, theme of life on a large city socio-literary front, ironic tone, short length." He is boasting because, in reality, he has done very little work on the book because of inertia caused by the fear that, once he writes it out, the dream of authorship will be over. He fears failure and would prefer to live with the illusion of future potential.

In a summary-form rendering, the reader is told that all of these initial episodes had happened a year ago; in the interim, the friendship between Kevin and Anna had developed into love. Kevin had once asked her to marry him, but she had refused. The action in the present then begins with a party given by Jasper Morrel, a phony who gives lavish parties for the local "literary" set. All of Jasper's parties promise a "big name"—a Dylan Thomas or a Truman Capote—as the main attraction; but these people never materialize. On this night, Dylan Thomas is to be the honored guest; but instead the only "famous writer" who shows up is Newton Bliss, author of "Chicken Gumbo," supposedly a musical comedy of the early 1930's.

The party scene is a caustic satire on the conversation of the "arty" types. After fragments of dialogue reveal the pretensions of the guests, the focus shifts to Newton Bliss, whose talents have recently been directed into writing patriotic and didactic songs in favor of God, country, and tolerance. He dominates the party with these songs and with his explanations of his theories of brotherhood: "all men are really shades of brown." (This facile optimist is another version of the Christopher Usher type seen in *The Oracle.*)

After the party, Kevin proposes again, and Anna agrees to be married to him soon. The next morning he tells his father, who congratulates him and inquires about his future plans. When Uncle Timothy hears about the planned wedding, he is furious that he wasn't consulted and that Kevin plans to marry a non-Catholic in a quiet service in the parish rectory. Uncle Timothy, who sees himself as the patriarch of the family, tries to arrange, through a Father Kinsella in the chancery office, for a wedding service in the cathedral by the bishop. Kevin rejects this idea, but feels guilty about disappointing Uncle Timothy again. The old patriarch had been disappointed several times earlier because Kevin didn't want to become a priest, didn't serve in combat when he was in the service, didn't want to enter the family business, and did the "silly, undignified" Little Simp comic strip.

In the meantime, interspersed scenes at the newspaper office show Burbank at work, and the managing editor visits Amos

Force's home for dinner and an evening of television afterwards; this material is used almost verbatim in *The Last Hurrah*. Kevin and Anna plan their wedding and talk about their religious differences, about conversions, and about what it is "to be a good Catholic." In separate scenes, Kevin talks to his associates who have heard of his intended wedding; and each of them—the "arty" Jasper, the cynical Burbank, the authoritarian managing editor, the frugal Amos Force—offers advice appropriate to his personality. When Kevin gets home that night, he gets a call from the distraught Anna who tells him that Charles, her "dead" husband, is alive, has escaped from Russia, and is on the way home.

When Kevin meets Anna, they decide that nothing, not even her returning husband, will change their love or their plans to get married. After some talk, Kevin slowly realizes that this decision will mean a divorce for Anna; and for him—according to his religious beliefs—to marry her would mean excommunication from the Catholic Church: he would be "living in adultery" with a woman who is still married. Nevertheless, Kevin proceeds with his plans to be married.

Kevin's father reacts strongly to this decision with great disapproval and disappointment. Charles Archibald returns, to resume living with Anna. When Kevin confronts Charles, a bland, unemotional man, Charles is quite neutral and understanding about Anna's previous relationship with Kevin; but he quietly informs Kevin that everything has changed. Anna, switching her loyalties, asks for Kevin's forgiveness when she tells him that her old affection for her husband has returned. Kevin leaves, crushed not only by Anna's refusal, but also by the fact that he has lost to such a mediocre rival.

The rejected Kevin returns home to tell his father about this turn of events. In a scene of "paternal correction," or "fatherly counsel," Kevin's father points out that Kevin has been weak—"drifting, following the line of least resistance." The father continues his correction by criticizing Kevin's "arty" friends and his attitude toward his work: "You know what you're doing is worthless and yet you continue. For five years of truly staggering fidelity, you've drawn that idiot boy with his idiot adventures." Anna, the father charges, was only the catalyst for Kevin's weakness to show forth in full flower. The father points out that Kevin seeks the easy way, that he was even willing to repudiate his religion, and that he lacks self-denial. "In the initial responsibility for this, my boy," the father says, "I am guilty, perhaps more so than you. I should have spoken before; I should have bolstered you where you were weakest. I did not; my conception of the role of fatherhood was sadly inadequate. And so, my boy, I apologize to you. It remains only for me to see if some amends can be made."

Humiliated, Kevin feels that "the indictment was severe, but not unkind. . . . My father had been troubled not triumphant." Kevin sees the words of his father as an incisive but warm criticism: nevertheless, he feels that his father has a "disproportionate alarm" over the son's weaknesses. He sees his own inertia as "not quite that desperate; damaging but not fatal." When, in rebuttal, Kevin says that he had not really intended to leave the Catholic Church, his father focuses on Kevin's ambition as a writer, telling him: "You've no spirit of dedication to the more important. You've allowed yourself to be submerged in the lesser, the work for which you have no respect. That's the sell-out of ability, of talent, of one's self."

Kevin then responds with a sharp criticism of his father's own failure—his lackluster attitude toward the presidency of the college and his easy compromise with the college's mediocrity. The father, sharply hurt, reveals his own sense of failure, of unfulfilled promise, and confesses his own errors of past rationalizations for his action: "I stand as a living illustration of all I've warned you against. I am a weak man." Kevin and his father are reconciled, and his father advises him to start a new life, to make a clean break by leaving his job and the city.

Kevin starts winding up the Litte Simp comic strip, planning to end the series and to leave the city. However, the managing editor brings Kevin the news that the paper's Sunday edition will no longer use Little Simp but that Kevin will still receive the same salary for his new workload, reduced now by half, because of the insistence of old Amos Force. As Kevin is weighing the implications of this news, Jasper calls to invite him to a party at which Dylan Thomas will *definitely* be; Kevin declines, and decides that he can make an effective compromise by staying in the city and continuing his reduced work on Little Simp, if he can stay away from his "arty" friends and devote more time to his novel. The manuscript ends with Kevin's determination to write his novel: "with the knowledge that whatever my father had

said, I would work, I would finish my book, I would come
through it all just as I had always planned."

Shortly after completing this manuscript, Edwin O'Connor began the intense, four-year-writing of *The Last Hurrah*.

CHAPTER *5*

The Last Hurrah

I *Background*

BY the time that Edwin O'Connor began writing *The Last Hurrah*, he had published one novel (*The Oracle*), had attempted three others, ("Luther Sudworth," "Anthony Cantwell," and "A Young Man of Promise"), had produced a long autobiographical narrative (the "Coast Guard" manuscript), had written dozens of articles and short stories, and had supported himself as a free-lance writer for nearly a decade. The long apprenticeship was over when he finally grasped the story he wanted to tell about the Irish in America. With great enthusiasm, he started writing the novel which he felt certain was to be a success. While economic necessity forced him to keep his part-time job as a newspaper critic (the "Roger Swift" columns) and as an editor (the Fred Allen scripts), O'Connor intensified his efforts on his own writing.

Later, when O'Connor was interviewed (*New York Herald Tribune*, February 5, 1956, 2) as to the origins of his ideas for *The Last Hurrah*, he attributed it to a long-standing curiosity: "I got interested in the political setup of an American city when in the Coast Guard during the war. My station happened to be Boston. Before that I had been at Notre Dame with the sons of some Chicago politicians, and I suppose that started it." When asked where he got his political insight, O'Connor replied: "As Henry James said, you don't have to live in a barracks to know about soldiers. You need a little intelligence and creative imagination. You know a little, and imagine the rest. You concentrate for a short time, absorbing it through the pores. And maybe, because nobody else knows much about it either, they'll say it's o.k. All I really wanted to do was to write a novel about human beings in politics." Certainly his association with Louis Brems was important in providing O'Connor with a wealth of folklore about big city politics, but afterwards O'Connor did not directly follow up this avenue of interest; in fact, he commented later that he had never been inside the State House, which was just a few doors away from his apartment. As Schlesinger (p. 9) wrote, "Ed was not greatly interested in politics *per se*. He had never worked in an election, had never been a political reporter, and did not make any systematic effort to interview or hang about with politicians."

In any event, O'Connor's interest in any kind of a political novel lay dormant for years. He had shown previous concern for the conflict between changing generations, but exactly *when* or *how* he conceived of Skeffington and the political story as his subject is vague. O'Connor never recorded that moment when he grasped the idea of Skeffington, but certainly that was the catalytic moment which brought everything together. Reasonably, it can be deduced that this took place as he was finishing, or had just finished, "A Young Man of Promise." Friends recall the great excitement O'Connor evidenced as he began to work on his new book, confident that he had a winner.

Consciously, O'Connor borrowed many things from the "Young Man of Promise" manuscript (the newspaper scenes, including Burbank, Amos Force, the managing editor, the Little Simp cartoon episodes; and minor characters, such as Uncle Timothy, the "amateur theologian" who appears as Roger Sugrue), and from two unpublished short stories: "C.B" (a character akin to Charlie Hennessey) and "De Mortuis" (the Knocko Minihan wake scene, and the politician-uncle and the observer-nephew relationship). Perhaps less consciously, O'Connor was rescoring themes first introduced in *The Oracle*: the flamboyant rogue, the word manipulator, the *old* man, and the private life of the public hero.

Working feverishly under the pressure of this new self-imposed goal, O'Connor suffered a near-fatal ulcer hemorrhage in January, 1953. O'Connor was stricken while writing, alone in the boarding-house, and was barely able to stagger down the hall to make an emergency telephone call. Rushed to the hospital, apparently dying, he received the Last Rites. The seriousness of his condition required a massive transfusion program; his friends at the *Atlantic* quickly organized a corps of blood donors which was able to provide an adequate supply of blood for the necessary transfusions. After the immediate crisis passed, O'Connor decided to use his small savings, which he had recently earned from the royalties on *The Oracle,* to finance a trip to Ireland. There he planned to continue writing his new book, but at a more leisurely pace. He was interested, he said later, "to see whether they had the same type of politician. I thought I'd better get at the roots of this thing, if I could." But eventually he perceived more of the differences and the misconceptions that the Irish and the Irish-Americans had of each other.

Seeking current information about Ireland, O'Connor introduced himself to Professor John V. Kelleher, the Harvard professor of Irish Literature. This meeting began a significant life-long friendship with Kelleher; later, O'Connor read all of the draft chapters of *The Last Hurrah* to Kelleher for his reactions, but at this early meeting Kelleher arranged for O'Connor to meet the Montgomery family in Dublin. The Montgomerys, a remarkable couple of great warmth and diverse artistic interests, befriended O'Connor while he was in Ireland; and to them *The Last Hurrah* is dedicated: "For Hop and Niall." Financially, O'Connor exhausted his meager savings while in Dublin and was forced to write to Edward Weeks asking for a one-hundred-dollar advance on future *Atlantic* articles. When Weeks sent him the check, O'Connor was able to survive in Dublin.

In January, 1955, O'Connor submitted the manuscript, originally titled "Not Moisten An Eye," in time for the competition for the Atlantic Prize, a deadline which he had been rushing to meet in the previous few months. Those who first read the manuscript rejected it; fortunately, the second reading was done by Esther Yntema who recommended it enthusiastically with an incisive, detailed report. She argued that the book was "profoundly moving," had great scope, and was a tour-de-force of an era passing. Of Skeffington, she wrote that he "is drawn large in scale (as if in an Egyptian painting, with the king twice the size of his attendants) . . . a magnetic figure, half-hero, half-rascal." Calling the novel a "vastly readable book," she saw the importance of the dialogue: "the talk—the endless, various, garrulous, vituperative, sentimental, funny, bombastic Irish talk." This two-page editorial report saved the day for O'Connor, for it put the book back into the judges' consideration; and it won the Atlantic Prize of five thousand dollars.

In February, 1956, *The Last Hurrah* was published; by October, the book had gone through fifteen printings in hardcover (300,000+); in the following years, paperback sales would exceed a million copies. In addition, the novel was selected for the Book-of-the-Month Club, the Reader's Digest Condensed Books (for which O'Connor received $80,000 to salve the pain of seeing it pruned), and various smaller book clubs. Columbia Pictures bought the movie rights for $150,000. Without exaggeration, there was a rags-to-riches Horatio Alger quality to O'Connor's experience. Within weeks, an unknown writer had become a best-selling author. And a new phrase—"last hurrah"—had entered our language. According to F. Stuart Crawford of the G. & C. Merriam Company, publishers of *Webster's Third International Dictionary*, who has supplied me with a dozen recent examples from their files, this phrase is now in common usage, usually suggesting "an intensive effort," a "swansong," or the ballyhoo of old-time politics.

II   *The Novel*

The Last Hurrah is the story of Frank Skeffington, the seventy-two-year-old mayor of "the City," who decides to run once more for office, an election which is to be his final gesture, the "last hurrah" of an old-style political boss. But the novel is more than an account of a political campaign, although the central action revolves around it; more than a dramatized sociological study, although the insights are keen ones into the changing generations of the immigrant children; more than a mere collection of delightful episodes and dialogues and characters, although the book is rich with humor and densely packed with memorable anecdotes and political folklore. In the midst of all of these qualities, the character of Frank Skeffington dominates the novel; larger than life, he is one of the truly unforgettable fictional creations of modern American literature. Skeffington, surrounded by his old cronies and in combat with his enemies, old and new, is "half rascal, half hero," an outrageously vital character who provokes a complex reaction from others, both within the story itself and without among the readers and critics of the novel.

The angle of narration is that of an omniscient narrator, but the auxiliary device that is used to reveal the complexities of Skeffington and the election campaign is the introduction of a confidant, Skeffington's nephew Adam Caufield, as an inside spectator. Adam's "neutral" stance, a mixture of sympathy and skepticism, makes him function as the reader's "representative." In structure, the novel is divided into four major sections: Part I (chapters 1–5), the introduction of Skeffington, his decision to run, and the reactions of others; Part II (chapters 6–10), the campaign; Part III (chapters 11–12), the climax of the campaign; Part IV (chapters 13–14), the illness and death of Skeffington. Within each of the chapters, O'Connor has the tendency to write in rather clearly defined *scenes;* thus, while some chapters run as long as forty pages, there is no difficulty in following the plot. With Skeffington, the election, and Adam Caufield as the core of the novel, O'Connor is able to keep control of the plot; but, at the same time, through these many brief scenes, he provides a broad scope to the novel and creates the illusion of a crowded, complicated campaign, but does so without the reader's becoming lost.

The opening chapter begins with Skeffington's announcement that he will run for re-election. Woven into the first few pages of the text are many of the important details which are developed throughout the story: Skeffington's getting older, the rumors of his ill health, his determined foes (especially the newspaper), the difference between his private comments and his public statements, his fondness for his nephew Adam, his exaggerated manner, and his quick ironic wit in parrying the questions of the reporters. But the most important function of the early pages of the novel is to establish Skeffington's oratorical flamboyancy because some of his lines, later in the book, if not read with this *persona* and voice in mind, could appear pedantic, strained, or dull. However, once Skeffington's image is established, the pauses, inflections, and tones in his speech can be imagined by the reader.

To justify Skeffington's diction, several pages in the opening chapter focus on his daily ritual of reading poetry, "his morning custom for nearly fifty years." Such poetry-loving politicians are uncommon, it is true, in mid-century American politics, but they are not unknown; in national politics, Senator Everett Dirksen of Illinois had a vast treasury of poetic lines always available to him and his flamboyant oratory was a perpetual delight to television interviewers and audiences. In local politics, Boston's former mayor, James Michael Curley, was such a poetry lover;

he too had the habit of a daily poetry reading which provided him with a wide ranging store of poetic allusions. Skeffington's poetic moments are presented as a mixture of business and pleasure, as a liberal pursuit and as a practical one.

In demonstrating the effect of Skeffington's poetry reading in the political arena, an anecdote recalls his earlier battles with Festus "Mother" Garvey, thus introducing the first of the "comic grotesques" who appear throughout as minor characters. After introducing and demonstrating Skeffington's poetic abilities, the emphasis shifts to his rhetorical skills, his awareness of audience considerations, his knowledge of the tricks of the trade so that he knows when and where and how much of his poetry to use so that he doesn't antagonize his audience: "The trick was, he knew, to space the grand phrases properly, to use them always with an air of winking complicity; to suggest, in other words, an allowable erudition untinted by the dangerous streaks of self-inflation. It was quite a trick, but Skeffington could say, without conceit, that it was one which he had mastered years ago." From this emphasis on rhetorical strategy in his speeches, there is a smooth transition to his awareness of the importance of the names and titles of other people in his everyday dealings with them, in his letters, and in his personal contacts.

This leads directly to the next scene in which these skills in personal contacts are demonstrated as he goes to his office at city hall and meets the daily line-up of supplicants waiting for him. Although only two cases (Mrs. Rocco Santagata and Timsy Coughlin) are rendered in any detail, the scene has the illusion of suggesting the crowds and the variety of pleas which Skeffington encounters every day. This effect is partially accomplished by the summary analysis of the narration ("In every case something was needed: a job, a letter of introduction, medical care for an ailing wife, a low rent house, a pair of glasses, a transfer from one city department to another, a lawyer, a hardship discharge for a son in the army, money. It was all purest routine: Skeffington handled them all easily and with no hitches"); and it is partially accomplished by brief side-comments, within the two main interviews, which suggest the multiple complications of his job. O'Connor doesn't dwell on the sociological accuracy of these scenes; but, as the little dramas occur, the characters are all playing their accurate roles: the newer Italian immigrants are beginning to affect city hall, and the Yankee forces of law and order are holding a rear-guard action in Unitarian meeting halls.

The first chapter closes by switching the emphasis to Skeffington's personal life, especially his relation with his son, Francis, Jr. The father is shown as being "baffled and badly disappointed" with his son, a lazy thirty-seven-year-old bachelor whose only interest is in dancing. Skeffington's long-standing disappointment with Junior's pleasant blandness is revealed in fragmentary flashbacks that recall the earlier discussions in which Skeffington's gentle wife, now dead, had acted as a buffer between the uncomprehending father and the flaccid son for whom Skeffington had greater expectations. The father-son theme that is introduced is sustained throughout the novel.

The second chapter establishes Adam Caufield, Skeffington's nephew, as a suitable observer to the main political action of the book. The first of the three scenes in this chapter shows Adam and his young wife, Maeve, at home. Their names, of course, are symbolic, perhaps too bluntly so; for, as Thomas Eliot noted, Adam was "a most improbable name to be given by a sweet colleen, Frank Skeffington's sister, to any son of hers." Or, as Anthony West nudged readers with his elbow: "Adam and Maeve (get it? *Innocents*)"; and readers familiar with R. W. B. Lewis' *The American Adam* recognize that O'Connor is not the only American writer to utilize such Adamic allusions. Although Maeve has met Skeffington only once, at her wedding, she doesn't approve of him, primarily because she has been so deeply influenced by her father, Roger Sugrue, who is fanatically antagonistic to Skeffington. Devoted and loyal to her father, Maeve suspects that Skeffington's personal charms, evident at her wedding, are merely a clever mask or a devious trick. To keep a peaceful marriage, Adam and Maeve have thus far avoided any arguments about either Skeffington or Sugrue, but in Skeffington's announcement of his new campaign, Maeve senses a dangerous situation at home.

Adam, despite his blood relationship with Skeffington, is presented as an "neutral insider." To Adam, Skeffington is essentially an "interesting stranger." As a youth, Adam had never really known Skeffington; later, Adam had been away from the city for a long time and had neither been interested in politics nor had seen a Skeffington campaign; but now he is curious, but not committed. Adam's job as a cartoonist at the local newspaper not only gives him complete freedom of time and movement, but also puts him in contact with some of Skeffington's bitter enemies: Amos Force, the old Yankee publisher who has nurtured a grudge against Skeffington for years, and Burbank, a cynical journalist who had once written exposé articles about the mayor. But, despite the newspaper's anti-Skeffington bias, Adam retains his job and neutral role because he works on the periphery of the office, drawing the "Little Simp" comic strip.

"Little Simp" is a parody of the "Little Orphan Annie" comic strip. Little Simp, an orphan boy with eyes "twin circles of unimaginable vacuity," roams the world with his pet chipmunk, Daddy, and emerges innocent and victorious from his daily variety of disasters and catastrophes. The "Little Simp" adventures are given extensive treatment in this chapter, several paragraphs in three later chapters, and brief mention in three others. O'Connor can be faulted for dragging this albatross around; certainly the details of the "Little Simp" adventures, although they are cleverly satirical *per se,* do not seem to merit so much attention and do tend to distract from Skeffington's story. While possibly defensible as another avatar of the innocent-boob-victorious figure, this borrowing from the "Young Man of Promise" manuscript was less skillful than his re-working of the character of Burbank.

Burbank first appears as the embittered "contest editor" of the newspaper, a man who is a knowledgeable and amoral cynic. Later, Burbank's lowly position is explained as he reminisces about his past glory as a reporter writing venomous anti-Skeffington material. Years ago, when Skeffington had sued for libel and won a large settlement from the newspaper, Amos Force had made Burbank the scapegoat for this fiasco. Burbank, who has little love for his employer, still sees Skeffington as a crook; but he feels *simpático* toward him as an engaging and likable man. Burbank's main function is to provide, from an insider's viewpoint, the background information of the Skeffington-Force feud.

The third chapter presents Skeffington in his natural environment at city hall and introduces his lieutenants, Sam Weinberg and John Gorman. After the opening scene, in which the cabalistic atmosphere of the city hall is suggested by the knots of minor politicos in the hallways and the fragmentary listing of the routine work to be done, Skeffington meets with Weinberg and Gorman to plan the campaign. These two confidants constitute Skeffington's cabinet. Weinberg, an unobtrusive lawyer, is a shrewd political tactician, the only person to whom Skeffington "almost gave his trust." Gorman is the only powerful ward boss in a city which Skeffington has centralized by stripping the power away from the ward bosses; only Gorman's power went unchallenged by Skeffington. Fiercely loyal to his ward, single-minded, and without further ambitions, Gorman works as an ally, neither a rival nor a subordinate to Skeffington, who respects Gorman's limited territorial claim. An important sub-plot in the novel centers on Skeffington's efforts to keep his promises to Gorman regarding the needed bank loan to finance a housing project in Gorman's ward. In their initial strategy session, Skeffington, Weinberg, and Gorman survey the chances of the seven opposing candidates, eliminating four of them as serious contenders. Sensing that the other three will have to form some kind of coalition, Skeffington decides to await his opponents' moves.

The fourth chapter centers on Skeffington's invitation to Adam (thus, to the reader) to observe the inside workings of the campaign; a good plotting decision, the invitation is made here, after the appetite has been whetted, rather than in the opening pages. As Adam arrives at city hall, more of Skeffington's loyal followers are introduced; and chief among these is Ditto Boland, the simple-minded devotee who worshipfully imitates the words and actions of the mayor. The opening scene is crowded with ethnic types (Casimir Kowalski, Thomas Jefferson), with "comic grotesques" (the Murphy brothers, Clam Carey), and with characters from sub-plots (Burbank; Fats Citronella, the jazz idol of Francis, Jr.).

In the inner office, Skeffington tells Adam his version of the feud with Amos Force, which contrasts with Burbank's version which had emphasized the libel suit. "Your friends the journalists," Skeffington says, "are responsible for this curious myth that public men fall out over public issues." Rejecting the "experts'" analyses that the feud was caused by "religious differences, racial hatred, party quarrels, even tax abatements—what you care to name," Skeffington tells Adam the root cause of his hatred toward Amos Force: Skeffington's mother, who had worked as a young maid in the rich home of the Force family, had been fired for stealing food and had been publicly humiliated. Explaining the situation, Skeffington condones and defends the petty larceny of the poor immigrants as being justified and necessary considering the slave wages and oppressive conditions forced upon them by the established society in that era.

When Adam questions the longevity of the feud over such a seemingly slight issue, Skeffington again emphasizes the supreme importance of the *personal* aspects of political life as he knows it: "There are twenty men in the outer office right now who couldn't tell you at the point of a gun where I stood on the matter of low-cost public housing, but every last one of them would know to the day just when I moved from Devaney Street to the Avenue, or what year I took the trip to Bermuda with my mother, or what I said to our beloved Cardinal when he tried to grab a city parking lot as the site for a parochial school gymnasium."

Then Skeffington begins to put forth his proposition to Adam; carefully, afraid of losing Adam's favor, Skeffington invites him to be an inside spectator of the campaign. Skeffington talks about the great historical interest of the campaign and emphasizes that no strings are attached: Adam will not be *used* in any way, nor will he be expected to become involved or committed. Adam agrees to the proposal, and only later does he wonder what sort of problems his involvement might cause with Maeve. After Adam leaves, Skeffington ponders alone on his inner motive for inviting Adam as witness: "He had felt the growing desire to have someone of his own family observe him in the conduct of his last campaign." Immediately following, Skeffington again thinks, with disappointment, of his own son. Thus Adam is the substitute son for Skeffington's paternal feelings; and Adam, orphaned by an auto accident, finds a father-figure in Skeffington. The two form an ideal "father-son" relationship in which each party respects and freely chooses the other.

The fifth chapter has seven major scenes which depict the various reactions of others to Skeffington's decision to run again for office. Generally, the hostile and friendly reactions tend to alternate, or are juxtaposed, so that the contrast is heightened. After the introductory device, the opening scene takes place at the home of Amos Force, the cranky old newspaper publisher, who is being visited by his managing editor. Most of this scene in which Amos is caricaturized as being stingy, vindictive, reactionary in politics, saccharine in religious piety, and in which the idiotic television programs are satirized, has been taken almost verbatim from the "Young Man of Promise" manuscript; but the detailed instructions given by Amos for the anti-Skeffington attack in the newspaper has been added at the end. Naturally, the arguments Amos uses against Skeffington are weakened by this presentation of the old man's idiosyncrasies and by his spiteful personal vendetta, but not all of Skeffington's opponents are to be such straw men.

The next scene shows John Gorman at a dance sponsored by his ward organization. There he functions as leader, listening to supplicants and talking politics with his followers. The conversation with Teddy Moran, the contractor for the expected housing project, furthers the development of this sub-plot; and the talk with Camaratta foreshadows the power play which will eliminate this rival. Throughout the scene the emphasis is upon Gorman's concern for his limited domain and the personal loyalties involved in ward politics.

In the following scene the major attacks and defenses of Skeffington begin with the talk between the cardinal, the spiritual leader of most of the city's people, and his young secretary, a monsignor who is rather sympathetic to Skeffington. As they start discussing the mayor, the monsignor comments on his "exceptional ability"; the cardinal rejects these "wildly romantic notions" and attacks Skeffington's record as a "working municipal executive." Professionally speaking, the cardinal claims, Skeffington is "haphazard, inefficient, and dangerous." The monsignor, feeling that the cardinal may lack objectivity because of his many battles with Skeffington, points out the public loyalty which Skeffington commands. The cardinal rebuts this statement by saying that the people have been gulled and seduced, bribed and bought by the Santa Claus in city hall. The cardinal closes the discussion at this point, but the monsignor's interest remains because he realizes that some day he will inherit the fruits of the cardinal's quarrel with Skeffington; in later chapters, the discussion continues.

In the next scene, one of the most delightful sections of the book, "Mother" Garvey visits Charlie Hennessey's house. (O'Connor has recorded his reading of this scene; see bibliography.) The dialogue between these two eccentrics is hilariously funny, but in this madness several valid points are presented about Skeffington and his new opponent. Charlie Hennessey, who is most frequently alone at night (except for his many dogs sprawled around), roams through his house "at a joyous half-trot," whistles loudly, reads magazines to "keep up" with science, talks to himself on his tape recorder, and criticizes the television programs. But tonight, Garvey enters, raging about Skeffington's decision to run again for office; and Garvey asks Hennesey to support a coalition to support young Kevin McCluskey.

Garvey starts his attack by complaining about Skeffington as a "poem reader"; but Charlie, who is perennially a candidate against Skeffington, has nothing but praise and admiration for the mayor's poetic and rhetorical ability. However, Garvey, with the fanaticism of a true believer, cannot tolerate anything good to be said about Skeffington and pleads urgency: "For the love of God, will you listen a bit! . . . Here's the city goin' over the hill to the poorhouse, arse over teakettle, and that dirty devil runnin' for four more years . . . And what the hell are we doin' about it?" Responding to Garvey's urgent plea, Charlie comments that Garvey has a twitching vein in his head and proceeds to give several exotic cures for high blood pressure. Garvey continues about Skeffington's greed and corruption, but Charlie defends Skeffington as not being motivated by personal gain and as a most generous man. After turning down the invitation to join the coalition, Charlie Hennessey then begins mocking the mediocrity of their candidate, Kevin McCluskey: "no capacity whatsoever . . . . mediocre . . . . undistinguished . . . . nothing upstairs but a mass of floating custard . . . . a grand young man, but simple." The enraged Garvey leaves, and Charlie returns to his "experiments."

The response of Nathaniel Gardiner is shown in the next scene. Gardiner, an aristocratic philanthropist, a man of ability, wealth, and social position, is an admirable representative of the old Yankee establishment. Gardiner, in speaking with his son, recognizes that Skeffington is a rogue and has many drawbacks; but Gardiner does have some sympathy for Skeffington, perhaps because both men share some of the same values: a sense of duty, a love for the city, and a passionate commitment. Gardiner objects to "these neutral tolerant times," and he admires Skeffington's vigor, boldness, and bravado. Despite the evidence of graft and corruption, Gardiner points out that Skeffington has accomplished many needed social reforms—slum clearance, health and recreational facilities. Although Gardiner would not endorse Skeffington now, he cautions his son to see both sides of the coin, to perceive Skeffington's virtues and to recognize the partiality and vindictiveness of some of his opponents.

The following scene shows Adam Caufield at a party that night speaking with Jack Mangan, an A.D.A. type, a young-sophisti-cated-intellectual liberal. Mangan considers himself a political analyst, and he predicts that Skeffington will lose the election because the old-style politics is passing away. The final portion of the chapter is devoted to Skeffington's actions on the evening of his public announcement. With Cuke Gillen, the official city greeter (modeled on O'Connor's friend, Louis Brems), and his other aides, Skeffington visits a memorial banquet for Eddie Mc-Laughlin. In honor of the dead man, Skeffington gives a eulogy which subtly turns into a political speech. Throughout the scene the emphasis is on Skeffington's rhetorical ability and his mastery of the manipulative tricks of the trade, skills demonstrated in the eulogy he delivers. Afterwards, home alone, Skeffington is satis-fied with the day, except for his disappointment with his son who did not bother to be with him as he had requested. The chapter closes with Francis, Jr.'s, coming home late from an evening of dancing, and his suddenly remembering that his father had wanted to see him about something that day: "He wondered if it were anything important."

This chapter concludes Part I (chapters 1–5): all major charac-ters have been introduced; the locale and background have been established; the complications have begun on the main plot (the election) and on the various sub-plots (the father-son relation, Skeffington and Adam, Skeffington's age and hints of illness, the housing project in Gorman's ward, etc.), and some of the various complicities among characters have been suggested. All of the action, which has taken place in one day, has been presented in regular sequence (morning, lunch, evening).

Part II (chapters 6–10) takes place several weeks later in the middle of the campaign. After a summary rendering of Skeffing-ton's activity in the interim, Chapter Six is divided into three major scenes: Adam's problems at home; Skeffington's blackmail of Norman Cass, Sr.; and a Skeffington strategy meeting with Weinberg and Gorman.

So far, Adam has not told Maeve of his promise to witness Skeffington's campaign, nor has he talked again with his uncle. Afraid of getting too involved, Adam has not acted. When his father-in-law, Roger Sugrue, dines with the couple, Adam is almost drawn into an argument about Skeffington. Sugrue, a successful self-made man and the owner of a chain of lingerie shops, feels qualified to be a self-appointed expert in politics, especially about Skeffington, and in religion: "As an amateur theologian he had acquired the passion for nosing about through diocesan affairs which sometimes affects the well-to-do Catholic layman." The argument over Skeffington is diverted by Maeve, but the scene indicates the growing tension within this family trio.

The episode in which Skeffington blackmails Norman Cass, Sr., is a well-plotted sequence which weaves together two of the subplots: the bank loan for housing in Gorman's ward, and the father-son theme. Norman Cass, Sr., the successful Yankee banker, also has a "worthless" son, a foil situation parallel to Skeffington's. Skeffington, aware of the personal motives of public men, exploits the banker's family pride by placing Cass, Jr., in a compromising position. With ironic flattery and witty cleverness, Skeffington has persuaded the son, a fatuous incompetent man of forty, to be the city's new fire commissioner. After the son has accepted and has signed the official documents, Skeffington takes the papers to the banker's office to ask for the housing loan necessary for Gorman's ward. Cass, Sr., in control of the money, refuses. Skeffington parries and feints with the banker at first, but finally reveals his blackmail scheme. If the loan is refused, Cass, Jr., will be publicly appointed; both Skeffington and Cass, Sr., know that it would be only a matter of time before the foolish son would disgrace himself by his own incompetency, and Skeffington would be forced to fire him. Cass accuses Skeffington of playing dirty pool, but the mayor responds with a tough attack upon Cass as a heartless slumlord and exploiter of the poor. To avoid the family's humiliation, Cass succumbs to Skeffington's blackmail and agrees to approve the loan. After Skeffington leaves, the angry banker vents his rage on his hapless son.

Skeffington reports his victory to his friends at the campaign strategy session and then proceeds to lay out the plans for their

attack on Kevin McCluskey, the coalition candidate opposing
him. Skeffington's basic maneuver will be to expose McCluskey
as a puppet, as the pliable tool of others. To support these efforts,
Skeffington reviews his financial tithing system; the campaign will
be financed primarily through money received as kickbacks from
the job patronage and contracts dispensed by city hall.

Chapter Seven, which is very brief, has the main function of
bringing Adam in as the observer. Uninvited by Skeffington to
the formal opening of the campaign, Adam watches Skeffington's
speech on television, thinking that Skeffington had forgotten his
earlier invitation to him. Working on the "Little Simp" cartoon
the next day in the office, Adam meets Burbank, drunk, who has
resigned from the paper to accept Skeffington's casual offer of
employment. When Skeffington finally calls Adam to invite him
to accompany him the next evening, the mayor explains that he
didn't consider the formal opening speech worth Adam's attention. Adam is pleased by this renewed contact at Skeffington's
initiative, but he is momentarily disturbed when Skeffington ac-
cidentally reveals that he had forgotten about his earlier promise
to Burbank.

Chapter Eight, a richly extended chapter, takes place at
Knocko Minihan's wake; and for it, O'Connor borrowed extensively from his unpublished short story, "De Mortuis," for the
opening pages and then worked in the details of Skeffington's
politics. Skeffington has invited Adam to observe him in action
at the wake; Adam is surprised at the invitation, but Skeffington
reassures him that he will learn something. When they arrive at
the house, Skeffington excuses himself in order to visit the widow
alone and leaves Adam in the parlor with Delia Boylan. Delia,
the talkative crone, is a standard participant at all Irish wakes;
she is one of O'Connor's best minor characters and rings so true
to a type that O'Connor received scores of letters from readers
who claimed that Delia was "just like" their Aunt Hannah or
their Aunt Molly. Delia, as guide, introduces Adam to all the incoming visitors and gives him a quick summation of their peculi-
arities.

Meanwhile, Skeffington is in the kitchen talking with the
widow Gert. Unknown to her, the mourners for her unpopular
husband have been summoned that evening by Skeffington as a
courtesy to her. Skeffington has also provided the food from the

city hospital, and he will intimidate the obsequious undertaker to lower his burial fee by a veiled threat of taking away his license. Skeffington gives Gert a thousand dollars, with a slight cover story which enables the widow to accept the money without losing her dignity. Such consideration and generosity on Skeffington's part should not be interpreted as a base attempt to win a few votes; after all, everyone at the wake is already part of Skeffington's tribe. But these actions do illuminate the attitudes of benevolent paternalism, of taking care of "one of ours," which indeed were strong forces in the old politics.

As Adam wanders through the crowd, talking to the mourners, it becomes apparent to him that no one is interested in the dead man; instead, the talk revolves around politics, especially the coming campaign. The sensitive Adam is shocked by what he considers to be a crass political manipulation of these funeral services. Most of the chapter is then spent in various ways of explaining, defending, and justifying these tribal rites and customs to Adam, the outsider. For example, the theme is introduced by an anecdote, seemingly unrelated, about Danno Herlihy's wake which was disrupted by his brother's appendicitis attack: "The family never forgave him. . . . The bum was a flycatcher, a scene stealer. He tried to cop the act at his own brother's wake." To Adam, at first, Skeffington seems to be a *scene stealer:* "Adam could not help marveling at the completeness of Knocko's failure to dominate, or even to intrude upon, his own wake. Here in the antechamber he was playing a bad second fiddle to the swapped vote and the living Skeffington."

Adam directly confronts John Gorman with the question about Skeffington's presence at the wake. The normally reticent Gorman responds with a long, serious lecture to Adam in which the old politician paternally admonishes the younger man: "You're a bit hard on your uncle, I think. The man has no need to go to wakes if he wants to collect a crowd about him; he can do that anywhere. . . . What he came here for tonight is simple as simple can be: he came to bring a crowd to Knocko's wake so the widow would feel a little better."

As Gorman finishes his analysis of the crowd, Charlie Henessey arrives to state the same ideas but with humorous flippancy. Then Charlie steals this scene as he begins explaining his latest scheme about a self-developing camera to take daily pictures of hospital patients to record their progress. Skeffington enters the crowd and banters freely with Charlie as Charlie pays homage to his rival for office: "Remember that while he may be a bum administrator, we have to admit two things about him. One, he has a grand heart, and two, he's the greatest orator and crowd psychologist that this part of the world has ever produced! . . . A terrible mayor but a great entertainer." As Skeffington enjoys Charlie's speech, it occurs to him that they share the same background and traditions and, to a great extent, the same gifts; but "somewhere along the line someone had forgotten to tighten a necessary wire, and the result was Charlie. Charlie with all his volcanic but essentially purposeless eloquence, his thousand and one unrelated interests, his wild, undisciplined, quixotic pursuit of impossible ends! Looking at Charlie in full flight was for Skeffington a little like looking into a mirror in a fun house: through the lunatic distortions, he could always manage to discern just a little of himself."

Later, when Skeffington and Adam are alone, Adam tells of his previous misgivings about the intrusion of politics at the wake; and he repeats what Gorman had told him. Skeffington responds by recreating accurately what he thinks Charlie Hennessey had to say, but he then presents his own attitudes about the affair and describes his own self-image: "I'm not just an elected official of the city; I'm a tribal chieftain as well." He reminisces about some of the tribal lore and customs of the Irish immigrants and about the former importance of the wake as a social gathering and a diversion away from the misery of their lives. He describes politics as the way "up the ladder" for the Irish, and he notes that, "whether I'd been there or not, they would have talked politics anyway." As the two men separate, Skeffington tells Adam (and the reader) that Adam's former misgivings about the wake were perfectly correct "from one point of view." "All I was concerned with doing," continues Skeffington, "was to show you another point of view." After parting, Skeffington speaks briefly with his son as the chapter ends; and Adam thinks about Maeve. Chapter Nine is a brief interlude chapter which ties up the loose ends of the Adam-Maeve complication. Maeve unexpectedly endorses Adam's association with the Skeffington campaign; she explains that she had previously talked with her father who had encouraged her to approve of Adam's adventure. Roger Sugrue felt that such familiarity with Skeffington would breed contempt and that Adam would be able to recognize the evil underneath Skeffington's superficial charms.

Chapter Ten opens with Skeffington involved in a party discipline matter: Johnnie Byrne, a city councilman, has been philandering and is on the verge of being divorced and causing a scandal. Skeffington, stern and angry, wields his authority to judge and sentence Byrne: "you've done the one thing you can't do with our people and get away with it. You're a married man who's been fooling around with another woman." Skeffington repudiates Byrne; to the mayor, adultery is not one of the "genial sins." Some reviewers have objected to this scene, as if it were out of character for such an "immoral" man as Skeffington; but O'Connor is accurately portraying the ghetto Irish rigidity about sexual matters. E. M. Levine, in *The Irish and Irish Politicians* (University of Notre Dame Press, 1966), uses this Johnnie Byrne scene as a fictional illustration to accompany his factual presentation that "the other human shortcoming the Irish condemn as an unspeakable sin is marital infidelity, and all Irish politicians are fully cognizant of its general significance and how it can jeopardize a political career." (p. 193)

In a brief interlude, before the next scene, Skeffington rests in bed. Although the passage is short and without emphasis, two important foreshadowings appear as Skeffington thinks first about his health and then about the use of television in the campaign; for later both disasters are linked to these sources. Concerning television, Skeffington sees it as being a shortcut to the electorate; an essentially *secondary* approach, not so effective as "the direct and personal visit with the sign of recognition, the extended hand, the solicitous inquiry into family affairs, the donation of favor or promise of favor. It was this procedure, painstakingly accomplished, that had always been the heart of Skeffington's campaign; he did not change now."

The last part of the chapter, crowded with activity as Adam joins Skeffington's busy schedule, provides a panoramic view of the city, its social and economic levels, its various ethnic groups, and its modern problems. Above all, however, this tour-de-force exhibits the many talents of Skeffington as an orator and as a politician as he adapts his message and style to the various audiences he encounters. Adam observes that "no two of Skeffington's expeditions correspond exactly; each had its distinct object, each was aimed at a special group of the electorate." Later, Adam realizes that he is "witnessing directly the chaotic diversity of the democratic process in action." Skeffington tells him that the secret is in making *compromises* among the various factions, and then illustrates his remark with the anecdote about the statue of Mother Cabrini.

After dealing with the regular suppliants at his office, Skeffington starts the tour with a visit to the radio station where he delivers, *ad lib,* a broadcast to the housewife audience listening; then to the waterfront, where one speech is geared to the commercial fishermen; another, a few minutes later, to the longshoremen. As luncheon speaker at the Audubon Society, his speech to the ladies there differs vastly from his wharf appearances. In the afternoon, Skeffington confers with Weinberg and Gorman, while Adam works briefly at the office before rejoining his uncle to complete the day. Together again, Skeffington takes Adam to witness him perform at an open-air meeting, at a tea party, at a hospital, at two dinner banquets, at a television studio, and at two house parties. By day's end, Adam, exhausted, wonders how his old uncle can manage this fatiguing style of living. Skeffington remarks that "in politics, only a young man can afford to look tired," and then tells another one of his semi-fables, an anecdote about an eighty-year-old politician who was taped up and wired together to look good for his campaign photos.

Part III (chapters 11 and 12) describes the final week of the campaign. Thus far, the focus has been on Skeffington; in Chapter Eleven, McCluskey's campaign is treated. Such disproportionate space given to the two opponents indicates that this novel is about the *character* of Skeffington and not a political novel in which ideology or the conflict between opponents is central. If such conflict were central, it would be necessary to give a more equal balance to the sides—to elevate both protagonist and antagonist equally in order to create a suspenseful conflict. But there is no giant to match Skeffington; no opponent his equal. Perhaps the sheer number of minor opponents, like dogs wearying a lion to death, might be considered equal. But O'Connor does not give credit to the *coalition* of Skeffington's enemies; he is beaten by an almost impersonal force—time and changing attitudes. It is appropriate that McCluskey is a bland, pliable mediocrity. To have given McCluskey "equal time" would have been to personalize him, elevate him, whereas O'Connor kept him as a cipher. Skeffington could have been beaten by a McDermott (K. of C., W. W. II vet, 4 kids) or a McDonald (K. of C., W. W. II vet, 4 kids) or a McDonough (K. of C., W. W. II vet, 4 kids). The important thing is not the man, but the photogenic face and the rented dog, television, and the new era.

McCluskey's advisors have decided that his campaign will be waged with television in order to be at a safe remove from the public: "their hope of success lay in preserving a decent distance between him and the public. A certain amount of direct contact was, of course, unavoidable; any more than that would be, they felt, suicidal." Thus McCluskey carries his message to the people, daily and nightly, by an expensive saturation campaign on television. Most of these television shows originate from the living room of the McCluskey home where the handsome young man is surrounded by his attractive wife, four winsome children, and a rented Irish setter. A large painting of Pope Pius XII, hung there for the occasion by the Protestant banker Cass, is the most prominent background feature in the room. In this pleasant atmosphere, McCluskey daily answers the prepared questions asked him by an aide. O'Connor heightens the satire by writing this scene as if it were a television script complete with stage directions, cue lines, and so forth.

After showing one of the "At Home with Kevin McCluskey" broadcasts, O'Connor uses the same device (as in Chapter Five) of switching to seven sets of viewers to describe the reactions of others to McCluskey. No one is impressed by McCluskey; even his closest supporters have little illusions about their candidate. Mother Garvey is satisfied with McCluskey's "plasticity"; Norman Cass, Sr., sees him as "amenable to the proper handling," or malleable. Amos Force, the reactionary, is not quite so pleased because McCluskey pays some mild lip-service to liberal ideals; but Force recognizes McCluskey's value in stopping Skeffington. Nathaniel Gardiner is thoroughly disgusted, as is the old cardinal, who terms McCluskey a "mealy-mouthed, maneuverable piece of dough." The cardinal, angered by the vulgarity and banality of the program, complains to the monsignor: "Is he representative of what we have to offer? I have spent my life in establishing a system of diocesan schools, encouraging our people to send their children to them, to our Catholic colleges and universities? Is this the result? A McCluskey? . . . Are we mass-producing McCluskeys?" But, when the monsignor forces the cardinal to make a final judgment, the cardinal decides that a McCluskey is still better than a Skeffington. Jack Mangan, the young liberal, makes a few caustic comments about McCluskey's "Mumsy-Daddy at home" broadcasts, but he still argues that new ideas do not have a chance with the Skeffington regime. Charlie Hennessey, of course, has a heyday ridiculing "Nut Boy" McCluskey and his rented dog.

Following these scenes of audience reaction to McCluskey, Skeffington and Adam are seen talking alone. Skeffington is thinking about Adam's "behavior" during the campaign: "He had been observant but unobtrusive; he had asked no purposeless questions; he had followed along the complicated, alien trails with an alert, intelligent interest. Moreover, he had obviously found pleasure in his uncle's company, and from this Skeffington had derived an unexpected satisfaction." As he drives to Adam's house, Skeffington suddenly asks to visit with Maeve. Skeffington's long conversation with Maeve is casual, warm, and engaging; Adam recognizes that the mayor's stories of family and friends are especially selected to ingratiate himself with Maeve. Adam also senses the "hint of loneliness" about Skeffington and realizes that, in all of their time together, Skeffington had never mentioned his own son's name. Thus, again, another chapter uses its final section to reveal the private life of the public man.

Chapter Twelve takes place on election night. After leaving his office, Adam goes to the campaign headquarters, a barnlike room filled with blackboards, folding chairs, and telephones. Ditto Boland and Cuke Gillen converse with Adam as the crowd grows, and the noise and the activity are suggested by a mass of well-selected details. Here O'Connor draws from his storehouse of political folklore as the exuberant followers retell the favorite anecdotes from the good old days: Footsie McEntee, who voted seventeen times in one election; Father Fahey and the Reverend Mr. Payne, the bogus priest and bogus minister who provoked anti-Garvey votes by their guile, etc. Adam wonders how many of these legendary feats are really true.

The Skeffington clan gathers. Skeffington comes in with Weinberg and Gorman; Burbank arrives; even Francis, Jr., drops in for a moment before going to a dance. All watch and analyze the blackboard tally of votes coming in from the wards, a passing bit of Americana now outdated by computer projections based on one percent of the electorate five minutes after the polls have closed. The first hint of disaster comes when the alert Skeffington notices a slight decline in his victory margin in a safe precinct. Skeffington leaves the main room to confer with Weinberg and Gorman; sensing trouble, the men phone several precincts for their reports. Within a few pages of tightly written, suspenseful revelations written in the imagery of a war battle, O'Connor climaxes the election plot. Skeffington, the pro, reads the signs of his defeat before anyone else. When Weinberg and Gorman comprehend the situation, they immediately put the blame on "betrayal" or on "organizational weakness," the two traditional reasons for defeat. But Skeffington is stunned by size of the impending defeat, a veritable avalanche, and is unable to comprehend why it happened. When the knowledge of the defeat reaches Skeffington's supporters in the main room, the excitement of the evening is replaced by the awed silence of the crowd. In this stunned atmosphere, Skeffington makes the customary concession speech; then, with bravado, he announces his candidacy for governor in the fall elections.

Adam invites Skeffington home, but the mayor wishes to be alone and is chauffeured away. Asking the chauffeur to stop a mile away from home, Skeffington, as he walks alone on the street, is overwhelmed with emotion as he realizes that his defeat has made him an object of pity and compassion. Depressed and humiliated, enraged and frustrated, Skeffington broods about the defeat; and, as he reaches the stairs of his home, he collapses with a heart attack.

Part IV (chapters 13 and 14) presents the death and funeral of Skeffington; it offers a different vantage point for both the reader and the characters within the novel to judge Skeffington. Until now, Skeffington has been a "young" man in the sense that he is future-oriented, actively looking forward, living in a world of possibilities. After the heart attack, it becomes apparent to Skeffington and to all that he has reached the end of his rope. With this awareness of the immediacy of death and the lack of future, Skeffington returns in reverie to the past. Until now, Skeffington has been a potent political force to be reckoned with by his foes;

now his defeat and death have eliminated this factor from his opponents' considerations.

The opening section of Chapter Thirteen is concerned with the details of housekeeping and scheduling in the Skeffington home as the mayor lies abed gravely ill. Here, the father-son theme is emphasized as Francis, Jr., is too inept to do anything; and Adam must take charge of the household. Adam, the surrogate son, competently handles the situation and views Francis, Jr., with a condescending sympathy: "it was next to impossible, and seemed somehow unfair, to hold bitterness towards this pleasant, obviously well-intentioned man, who, although now approaching forty, revealed in every word the spirit of some growing and peculiarly ingenuous boy. It was Skeffington who, years before, and to his wife, had in a disgruntled moment summed up his son as 'a likable featherhead.' "

The second scene in the chapter veers away from the personal emphasis on Skeffington when Jack Mangan, the young liberal, visits Adam and gives his analysis of Skeffington's political defeat. Mangan discounts the coalition and the money of Skeffington's opponents; he claims that the real cause for the defeat is President Franklin D. Roosevelt. When William V. Shannon, in *The American Irish (1963)*, analyzes the career of Mayor James Michael Curley of Boston, he states that the usual explanation of Curley's eventual defeat was that the welfare state had outmoded the old style of politics; but Shannon's book offers other explanations for Curley's downfall. Curley's strength, he says, was "in his ability to define, dramatize, and play upon the discrimination, resentments, and frustrations suffered by the Irish community" and that these frictions had been lessened by the growth of a middle-class Irish group, by Curley's own election as Governor of Massachusetts, and by the scope of the economic depression. By detailing these causes, Shannon revises his earlier analysis of Curley's defeat, published in *The Reporter* of January 17, 1950, as not being an adequate explanation; but it seems probable that O'Connor used Shannon's article in *The Reporter* as a source for Jack Mangan's speech in the novel. Thus, Mangan's analysis may be considered adequate but not complete; in O'Connor's two later novels, he gives more attention to the changing generations, the younger middle-class Irish and their political attitudes.

The latter section of the chapter, sharply focused on Skeffington, has three movements: Skeffington's reveries of the past, the gathering of the friends, and the deathbed scene. In these passages, O'Connor's lyrical writing borders on poetry; indeed, Professor Charles Cŷr related that several years ago he had experimentally reset some of these paragraphs into the form of free verse. Later, the opening part of *All in the Family* achieves a similar lyrical quality in style.

As the dying Skeffington daydreams, these fragments of memory are carefully selected by him to avoid the betrayals, the defeats, and the unhappiness so that he can take pleasure in the thoughts of the happy days in the distant past. He remembers the comfort of his mother's love in his boyhood, the exhilaration of his first youthful speech and his first victory parade, the satisfaction derived from his clever manuevers against his enemies, the pleasurable comradeship of his old friends and followers, but most especially, he remembers Kate, a highly idealized version of the "good wife." Of the recent past, Skeffington's pleasant memories center on his nephew: "with fondness and contentment and affection; Adam became part of the sunlit, lingering daydream." As his reverie is ending, Skeffington again thinks of the city: "*his* city, the wonderful, old, sprawling chaos of a city. . . ."

In the afternoon, the clan of Skeffington's close associates begins to gather; and, from this point on, the archetypal patterns of the "death of the hero-king" are very strong. Almost in tableau fashion, the court jesters (Ditto, Cuke Gillen), the wise old men (Weinberg, Gorman), the young squire (Adam), and the priest (Monsignor Burke) come to apotheosize the dying king. Skeffington asks Ditto and Cuke for their advice about running for governor, then listens attentively to their recommendations. Adam understands Skeffington's intention in this "burlesque council of war:" it is a final act of kindness to his enthusiastic, albeit limited, friends. "It was a game: Skeffington had summoned them here today to play the parts they loved the best; now that it no longer mattered, they had become the counsellors to the king." The wise Weinberg and Gorman speak briefly and solemnly before Skeffington relapses into sleep; sensing the end is near, Adam sends for Francis, Jr., and for Monsignor Burke. The priest arrives to give the Last Rites, but Skeffington's son cannot be located.

As Skeffington's life begins to ebb, Maeve and her father, Roger Sugrue, enter the room. As an unwelcome representative of the enemy camp, Sugrue, speaking to the priest, smugly remarks that Skeffington "knowing what he knows now, if he had to do it all over again, there's not the slightest doubt but that he'd do it all very, very differently!" At this, Skeffington stirs, forcing out a reply: "*The hell I would!*" The grand gesture, the swan song: "The words came out in a hoarse whisper, but they were loud, distinct, confident and undefeated. Adam felt like cheering. He heard the Monsignor exclaim, softly and delightedly, 'Oh grand, grand, grand!'" Dorothy Millais (a former student of mine) has incisively suggested that perhaps Skeffington's themes can be reduced to his three key simple sentences: "*I want to.*" (His stated motive for the campaign.); "*I have to.*" (His endurance in it.); and "*The hell I would!*"

Skeffington asks for his son, then smiles and winks at Adam, and dies. If the reader is emotionally stirred by this chapter, one ought to reflect on the validity of such a reaction, on the writer's skill necessary to evoke such reaction to a fictional character, and on the possible contrary state of being neutral or unmoved by these scenes.

Chapter Fourteen, the final chapter, is structured in three major sections: the funeral, the reactions of others to Skeffington's death, and the friends at the cemetery. After a summary rendering of the three-day wake in which Skeffington lies in state for the thousands of mourners who file by, the funeral service in church is rendered more fully. Here the narration alternates between descriptions of the solemn liturgical rites and of the variety of mourners within the church. The eulogy, delivered by Monsignor Burke, concentrates on Skeffington's personal qualities and disclaims specific judgments about his public life, although the monsignor's "neutrality" certainly leans in Skeffington's favor.

Afterwards, the same characters, whose reactions have been surveyed twice before, make their final statements about Skeffington. The comments of some of them are merely appropriate, true to form, or repetitious of earlier attitudes: Mother Garvey, Amos Force, and Norman Cass, Sr., are spiteful still, sardonic, maliciously pleased at Skeffington's death; Charlie Hennessey is still praising Skeffington's warm heart and grand speech. But Nathaniel Gardiner's reaction and the discussion between the cardinal and the monsignor are of greater interest because they develop new insights into an evaluation of Skeffington's life.

Gardiner, whose objectivity has already been established, disagrees with the monsignor's eulogistic words because the priest "had left out too much." Gardiner's reflections on the "adroit and ruthless" political maneuvering of Skeffington emphasize that the mayor's entire career "seemed to have been devoted to the contravention of the law." In Gardiner's earlier scene, he had noted the specific instances of Skeffington's contributions to the social welfare of the city; now Gardiner specifies more clearly some of the corrupt practices. Yet, remembering Skeffington's wit, congeniality, charm, and good-humored audacity, Gardiner realizes that he both "liked and deplored" the man: "The old buccaneer, for all his faults, had at least been a capable, vivid, unforgettable personality; he had been succeeded by the spearhead of a generation of ciphers."

As the cardinal discusses Skeffington's eulogy with the young monsignor, the underlying motive for the cardinal's antagonism toward the mayor is revealed. Skeffington's great sin, thinks the cardinal, is that he has damaged the reputation of the Catholic Church. To the outside public, the mayor is "Skeffington, the Typical Irish Catholic Politician" and the cardinal vehemently states: "This man cheapened us forever at a time when we could have gained stature: I can never forgive him for that!" The cardinal's stated motive to protect the image of the Church may not really be the whole story, but it does ring true to the "altruistic" defense of the Faith made by a true believer and by the demand for organizational loyalty made by a chief executive.

At the cemetery, after Skeffington is lowered into the grave, the close friends talk briefly to one another before parting. Adam and Maeve give Francis, Jr., a ride back to his house; as they drive together, Adam realizes that a change has occurred in Skeffington's son: Francis, Jr., is going to face the reality of returning to the empty house; and Adam regards this fact as possibly a "good sign." There is the hint of hope for Francis, Jr.: now that his powerful father is dead, the younger man may perhaps become independent and mature. As Adam drives away, the kaleidoscopic memories of Skeffington overwhelm him with emotion. Later in the day, unable to work at the office, Adam catches a cab and drives by Skeffington's house. As they pass the house, the cab driver, representing the common man, tells Adam a story of Skeffington's kindness, twenty years ago, when the mayor had sent him an autographed "Babe Ruth" baseball for his son: "Whaddaya think of that? . . . What a great guy!" Adam sees Junior's light on in his room in the empty house, and in Adam's imagination "he could see the ghosts of the lines that had once formed at the door, and now would form no more." His pilgrimage over, Adam goes home.

The Last Hurrah received an enthusiastic popular response. Reviewers, too, were almost unanimous in their praise of the novel, or, at least major portions of it—the sense of vitality and scope, the sheer delight of the dialogue, and the character of Skeffington. However, three major patterns of interest can be extracted from the initial reviews: the question of Skeffington's relationship to James Michael Curley, the "Irishness" of the novel, and the "ethics" of Skeffington.

III *Frank Skeffington and James Michael Curley*

Practically every reviewer of *The Last Hurrah* felt it necessary to hint coyly that the character of Skeffington was based on the life of James Michael Curley, Boston's flamboyant political boss who was reelected mayor four times (serving part of a term while in a federal penitentiary) and elected once as governor of Massachusetts. Certainly colorful political bosses such as Curley had to exist as a source for this novel; but, as Schlesinger states, "the question whether Skeffington was based on James M. Curley is entirely trivial. Obviously in some early sense Curley suggested the idea of Skeffington . . . but the characters in the novel, as re-created in the author's imagination, departed extensively from the original. Curley, for example, was a mean-spirited and bitter man, with few of Skeffington's private charms." Definitely, the book was not a *roman à clef* of Curley's life or of an actual political campaign; O'Connor made no attempt to research the subject, to study the history of Boston politics, or to write a novel with a cast of identifiable personalities. In perspective, this now seems clear; but at the time of publication it was not so easily seen because of the unanticipated reaction of the aging James Michael Curley himself.

Curley, asked by a Boston newspaper to review the forthcoming novel, read *The Last Hurrah* and soon began to threaten

O'Connor with a libel suit. But, as the book's popularity increased and it became clear that the public was overwhelmingly sympathetic toward Skeffington, Curley's attitude became paradoxical. While continuing his threats of a lawsuit, Curley began to identify himself with Skeffington and to speak publicly (in lectures and interviews) about the novel as being *his* story. O'Connor constantly denied this claim, but the aged Curley, long inactive from public service, relished the limelight which the controversy focused on him. Several years after Curley died, O'Connor, writing in retrospect about these incidents in "James Michael Curley and *The Last Hurrah*" in the *Atlantic* of September, 1961, (48–50) recalled: "Over the last five years I have spent much time in denying that Frank Skeffington was a fictional version of the late Governor Curley. Not that it matters now, but he wasn't. For a long time I made periodic and dutiful efforts to convince people of this, but while some were convinced, others were not, and foremost among these was Governor Curley himself."

Although O'Connor's article treats the old politician quite kindly, O'Connor did get annoyed at the constant repetition of questioning from countless people who wanted to know if Skeffington "was *really* Curley." Such a question naturally obscured the imaginative talent needed by an author to create a fictional character, and it also revealed the questioner's lack of knowledge about Curley's political history. While such ignorance may have been excusable at the time *The Last Hurrah* was published, it no longer is a defensible ignorance since Curley published his autobiography, *I'd Do It Again* (1957). Curley titled his book with a phrase suggestive of Skeffington's deathbed statement ("The hell I would!"); but he does not recount the O'Connor affair except for one brief allusion in the final pages. However, the details of Curley's life and attitudes as told in this autobiography amply demonstrate how far O'Connor's portrayal of Skeffington departs from any *roman à clef* intention.

In contrast to those who would suggest too close a parallel between Skeffington and Curley are those readers who do not recognize O'Connor's use of certain aspects of Curley's career. Some critics have challenged the verisimilitude of Skeffington as a city boss. However, parts of Curley's record provide a defense for two "errors" attributed to O'Connor: first, some have argued that the centralized power which Skeffington held was not a "realistic" presentation of old-city politics in which the ward and precinct leaders, the party officials, and the party organization "really" held power more than any individual mayor; second, some have argued that Skeffington's indifference toward personal financial gain was an "unrealistic" picture of the graft-oriented city bosses. In these respects, William V. Shannon's chapter on "The Legend of Jim Curley" in *The American Irish* (1963) is a useful introduction to point out that Curley's reign in Boston, although *atypical* of city boss politics, did have these two "unrealistic" qualities. More recently, Mike Royko's *Boss* (1971)—a biography of Chicago's mayor, Richard J. Daley—notes a similar *atypical* concentration of power in one man, a politician apparently not motivated by personal financial gain.

Other characters in the novel were based, *partially*, on real Bostonians. As noted, O'Connor's friend Louis Brems provides the basis for Cuke Gillen; and the cardinal suggests Cardinal O'Connell. Schlesinger (p. 14) writes that Maurice Tobin "suggested the idea" of Kevin McCluskey but is "far less vapid and more independent" than the fictional character whom O'Connor used to symbolize blandness. The fictional philanthropist Nathaniel Gardiner was suggested by the life of Henry Lee Shattuck. The closest parallel to reality is found in the character of Charlie Hennessey, based on the eccentric Clem Norton. If nothing else, the "Curley affair" lends credence to *The Last Hurrah* as being a "realistic" political novel. It is amusing to note that O'Connor's publishers also received threats of libel suits from the kin of former politicians in Kansas City, Chicago, and Philadelphia.

As a "political novel," *The Last Hurrah* was widely accepted by experts of diverse political experience. Raymond Moley, of FDR's "Brain Trust," wrote in the *Los Angeles Times* of September 18, 1956, that he had long avoided reading this best-selling book because of his distaste for such novels "which are usually written by somebody who never knew a real boss and never fought a campaign." But, after reading *The Last Hurrah*, he raved: "the authenticity of the author's professional capacity comes out in the first dozen pages. The book's only rivals in the fictional literature of American politics have been the American Winston Churchill's *Coniston* and Brand Whitlock's short story, 'Malachi Nolan'." Arthur Schlesinger, Jr., and John Kenneth Galbraith, both closely associated with the Kennedy administration, have praised the novel highly. Schlesinger (p. 14) stated that it is "properly regarded as the best American novel about urban politics," and Galbraith has related that the book's appeal is not limited to American politicians alone. Galbraith, as American ambassador to India, gave a copy to Prime Minister Nehru, who later told him that it was "the best political noved he had ever read." Galbraith (in a letter to me,) stated: "I certainly think that Edwin O'Connor is a writer of first rate importance. The political novel has always been a source of difficulty for writers. Very few have mastered it and there can be no question that *The Last Hurrah* is one of the rare and important examples of such mastery."

Joseph Blotner, in *The Modern American Political Novel* (1966) discusses *The Last Hurrah* in the context of some 140 political novels published in the twentieth century. Blotner places *The Last Hurrah* into one of the archetypal patterns ("The Boss") which he has observed in his study and criticizes parts of the novel. He is especially disappointed by O'Connor's "dilemma," the "unresolved ambivalence" toward Skeffington which Blotner feels "weakens the novel." But, despite these comments, Blotner admits that "*The Last Hurrah* is the most absorbing of the novels dealing with the Boss and one of the most interesting in the study. It is a problem for the critics to determine why it is not a better novel." Blotner is close to solving the "problem" himself; if one can appreciate, or at least tolerate, the legitimacy of "unresolved ambivalence," then *The Last Hurrah* does indeed become a "better novel."

IV The Irishness of The Last Hurrah

Before publication, O'Connor had anticipated that his novel would infuriate the Irish-American reader. John Kelleher, Professor of Irish Literature at Harvard, the friend to whom O'Connor had read all of the early drafts of the novel, recalled in his *Atlantic* memoir: "We were united, too, in one large miscalculation, expecting that he would be denounced by angry old priests from a thousand pulpits and that every Irish society in the country and most of the Holy Name Societies would pass resolutions condemning him for a dirty bird and a fouler of his own nest."

Unexpectedly, only one reviewer—Father Harold Gardiner in *America*, February 18, 1956—even suggested that Skeffington's "moronic followers" might "rub the wrong way with many Irish Catholics" (567). And, of the hundreds of letters received by O'Connor from his readers, only a handful were denunciations of his treatment of the Irish. Kelleher's explanation of this surprising turn noted that "Unbeknownst to us, unnoticed till then by anybody, the public humorlessness that settled down over the American Irish about the turn of the century when the Irish societies drove the Irish comedians off the stage had silently lifted. The Irish could laugh at themselves again. Unfortunately by that time there was not a hell of a lot left to laugh at."

Kelleher did the front page review for the *New York Times Book Review* of February 5, 1956, and he praised the novel: "The first successful Irish-American novel. . . . the whole essential Irish-American story here, every shade and facet of it. . . . the nearest yet to a good history of the Irish-American in full career." Granted, Kelleher was no neutral outsider reviewing the work, but his expertise in this area of literature is an important factor to consider. Kelleher begins by describing the existing dichotomy in Irish-American novels: on one hand, the "why God loves the Irish" novel with no real conflicts among all the lovable Irishmen; on the other hand, the more recent books "usually dominated by a gloomy sensitive young narrator whom we may call Studs Dedalus" who lives in a world of bigots and bums. In *The Last Hurrah*, he notes, there is conflict all over the place: "politician against politician, Irish against Yankee, lay leader against clerical leader, and the great final conflict in which Frank Skeffington, the big, utterly individual political boss, is overwhelmed by the newer generation as by a glacier of unflavored gelatin." In the dramatization of this conflict and in the triumph of the "generation of ciphers," the collective tragedy of the Irish is demonstrated as the wildly vigorous immigrant generations succumb to the "millennium of faint feeling and moral mush" typified by the bland young Irishman, Kevin McCluskey. But Kelleher points out that, while O'Connor certainly regrets the victory of McCluskey, "he is not at all sentimental about Skeffington. He has no doubts about what Skeffington cost the city or the Irish."

Kelleher described O'Connor's humor as "backward-looking," as working primarily in reminiscences and recollections of an age gone by. Certainly the dominant tone of *The Last Hurrah* comes from Skeffington's ironic wit, not from the farce or burlesque of the "comic relief" interludes of the eccentrics. Julian Moynahan, in the *New York Review of Books* of April 30, 1964, recognized this fact when he pointed out that "the characteristically somber atmosphere of his writing is anything but appropriate to the mode of straight comedy in which many of his admirers insist on pigeonholing practically all of his writing. For example, if *The Last Hurrah*—any of it—is 'hilarious' then the defenestration of the Earl of Gloucester in *King Lear* is a laff-riot. On the other hand, Skeffington's study does perfectly well as sad comedy, although I do believe that actual Boston is not and never was so dim and dreary as the prevailing tone and mood of *The Last Hurrah* make it seem."

Wherein does the "Irishness" of *The Last Hurrah* lie? Obviously, the characters and the situation (urban politics) are "Irish," but, beyond this superficial consideration, most reviewers have noted the *stylistic* qualities which are so appropriate to the subject matter. Howard Mumford Jones, in the *Saturday Review* of February 4, 1956, termed the novel "a triumph of style. O'Connor, with no attempt at Irish dialect of the Mr. Dooley variety, has caught the exact rhythm and ictus of Irish political speech." If, as *Time* in its February 13, 1956 issue claimed, O'Connor makes his novel ring with the harsh brogue of the Boston Irish, the important thing to notice is that this stylistic achievement is made through the rhythm of the sentence structure and paragraphing, and through the metaphoric language. Karl Schriftgiesser, in the *New York Herald Tribune* of February 5, 1956, made the important negative observation that "with a marvelously Celtic lilt of language. . . . there is not a phony 'begorrah' in all its 400-odd pages." This absence of "begorrahs" and the other clichés of Irish-American "dialect" writing indicates O'Connor's close attention to language and his good ear for recording authentic speech patterns; his dialogue is based on accurate observation, not on the stereotyped Pat-and-Mike dialect of an artificial tradition. The only character in the novel whose language comes close, deliberately, to the artificial dialect is the petulant "Mother" Garvey.

The only extended criticism of O'Connor's "Irishness" appears in Ronald J. Dunlavey's "Last Year's Hurrah" in *The New Re-*

public of March 25, 1957, in which he takes on a whole score of reviewers for their "enthusiastic hurray-for-the-Irish chorus rather than a serious invocation of critical norms." (16–17.) Dunlavey begins by conceding the merits of the novel as "Funny and nostalgic . . . sympathetic apologia . . . a needed and astringent satire on television political campaigning . . . some excellent Irish-American folk-humor"; but he then attacks both the novel and its reviewers. *The Last Hurrah*, Dunlavey claims, is inaccurate as a political and social commentary; it is filled with cardboard characters who "perpetuate the ancient and pitifully inaccurate tradition of the Irish as sentimental buffoons." Most of Dunlavey's criticism concerns Skeffington's "ethics," but his announced purpose, which he comes to in the last three paragraphs, is to rebut those who have hailed *The Last Hurrah* as "a great novel about the Irish-Americans."

Dunlavey argues that "O'Connor's depthless sketch of the City Boss as a kind of superior song-and-dance man mirrors a portrayal of the Irish-Americans as a class." Dunlavey claims that O'Connor deals in stereotypes:

Sometimes they are gentle, good-hearted folk, generous and innocent, with names like John and Kate and Molly. More often they are pratfalling buffoons, like the fabled eccentrics in the stories they tell each other—stories about 'Nutsy' McGrath (kicked to death by a camel), 'Clam' Carey (died from eating bad clams), 'Lumps' McGuire (killed when the trophy-room axe fell on his head), 'Billie' McGrath (sweated to death), Silly Jim Casey, Snapper Brady, Little Jim Callahan, Buster Maloney. After a while, the doings of these storied clowns can hardly be distinguished from those of the characters who talk about them—Ditto Boland, Delia Boylan, Cuke Gillen, Footsie McEntee, Tansy Cullen, Charlie Hennessey, Festus Garvey—and Skeffington himself.

From this premise, Dunlavey concludes that the characters of the novel are all "Irish saints or Irish comics" and that for O'Connor "to describe the Irish-American community almost exclusively in terms of sentimentality and low humor is as inaccurate as to describe it entirely in terms of Farrell's 'spiritual poverty'." Dunlavey summons up allusions to the "brutal genius" of Irish writers such as J. M. Synge, Sean O'Casey. Liam O'Flaherty, James Joyce, and Sean O'Faolain to point out their literary merits in

comparison with the stereotype of the "gay, pious, romantic, pug-
nacious Irishman" so beloved by Hollywood and Tin Pan Alley.
By implication, Edwin O'Connor's book apparently is considered
in the second category as Dunlavey hopes that someday a novelist
with "full awareness of his responsibility to his subject, his craft,
and his reader" will write the great Irish-American novel: "Otherwise, the result will be simply another commercial concoction—
entertaining and provenly profitable hokum, but hokum none the
less."

Several errors in Dunlavey's argument warrant analysis. His
concluding remarks about "commercial concoction" fall into the
familiar pattern of charges of commercialism leveled against
O'Connor as a penalty for his popular success. Such insinuations
about the motive of a writer and such lectures about "The Artist's
Responsibility" would best be left unsaid by any critic unaware
of the author's background and development. Dunlavey also falls
into the error, made most commonly by reviewers sympathetic to
O'Connor, of overextending the scope of the book: *The Last
Hurrah* is not the definitive book about "the Irish-American community." The novel is about Frank Skeffington's world, city-hall
politics, which captures a great deal of the spirit of the community; and neither O'Connor nor his publisher's blurbs ever went
as far as some of his enthusiastic readers did in their claims which
apparently provoked Dunlavey's response.

Dunlavey's list of "Irish comics"—a catalogue of names which
lumps together the protagonist with the auxiliary characters and
the anecdotal characters—errs by not discriminating the *proportion* given to each in the novel. First, the "cosmic grotesques"
("Nutsy" McGrath, etc.) of the anecdotes merit only a few lines;
the functional auxiliary characters (Cuke Gillen, etc.) get only
a few pages; the overwhelming proportion of the book belongs
to Skeffington. Second, the speech and attitudes of the auxiliary
characters are not indistinguishable from one another as Dunlavey suggests: Mother Garvey's bitter complaints differ as widely
from Charlie Hennessey's zany optimism as Cuke Gillen's efficient
advice differs from Ditto Boland's simple idolatry. More important to note is the rich variety of tones and attitudes in Skeffington's speech as he talks to foe and friend, in public and in private.
Although Skeffington's subtle, sarcastic irony predominates, he
has a whole range of voices within the novel.

Dunlavey's concern is legitimate; other serious Irish-American scholars and organizations (such as the Irish-American Cultural Institute) have long fought against the stage-Irish stereotypes, the chauvinism, and the artificial exploitation (especially of St. Patrick's Day) which degrade the Celtic cultural heritage. O'Connor himself shared such a scorn for the "professional Irishman"; as Kelleher noted in his *Atlantic* memoir (p. 51): "Many indeed were the men and slogans on which he turned a bleak eye: the God-love-you-boy-and-keep-the-faith kind of Irishman with a heart like an ice cube." Later, in *All in the Family*, O'Connor's disdain for the Irish-American chauvinist is more apparent, especially in the invectives hurled by Uncle Jimmy against the "Super-Harps," the "Cornball Harps," and even "the home-grown Micks." O'Connor was not a dealer in plastic shamrocks, shillelaghs, and Blarney Stones; nor was he an impish leprechaun chirping "top of the morning to ya." In all probability, Dunlavey and O'Connor would have agreed about their basic attitude toward the Irish in literature.

V   *The Ethics of Skeffington*

Any serious evaluation of *The Last Hurrah* must eventually focus on the character of Frank Skeffington, the heroic-size protagonist who dominates the novel. Most reviewers agreed with the publisher's advertisement that Skeffington was "half hero, half rascal," and the majority regarded Skeffington as being somewhat romanticized. For example, the reviewer in the *Atlantic* of February, 1956, said that he "occasionally felt that the seamier facts of political life were presented in too benevolent a key" (80). *Time* of February 13, 1956, described Skeffington as "a lovable rogue—a combination of Santa Claus, Robin Hood, a Chinese warlord, and the late John Barrymore" and noted that O'Connor "may not always see his hero with 20-20 vision, but he does something even rarer among modern novelists—he makes him come alive, with love" (94). Father Gardiner, in *America* of February 18, 1966, wavered in his response to Skeffington, seeing him as "such a melange of good and bad that he strains one's credulity," yet noting that Skeffington "may have been unscrupulous, but he had style and charm and real ability" (568).

But a few reviewers went beyond such mild comments to wage

rather strong attacks on Skeffington's ethics. James Benet, in the *San Francisco Chronicle* of February 6, 1956, dismissed the book as "sentimental nonsense" about a corrupt political boss. Even stronger in his objection, Anthony West, in the *New Yorker* of February 11, 1956, felt that *The Last Hurrah* was a subversive novel: "One can imagine a powerful and convincing novel written tough-mindedly around the idea that the old-time city boss was a rococo ornament to the political scene and the source of a barrel of rough fun, but Mr. O'Connor's sentimental presentation of that barbaric figure as a fairy godmother of widows and orphans is more than hard to take. It persuasively pretends that mean vices are virtues, and it is that rare thing, a genuinely subversive book" (121–24).

Analyzing the scene at Knocko Minihan's wake, West considers the arguments defending Skeffington's actions to be specious justifications for theft so that Adam (and the reader) become "a consenting party to the robbery of the public till." West also charges that O'Connor blurs the distinction between the dishonesty of "some businessmen" and the dishonesty of a public official: "Mr. O'Connor is saying that Cass and Skeffington differ only in that the first is a bigger hypocrite than the second, and that no distinction be drawn between the traditional New England Puritan ethics of the one and the chiseling city-hall operator's outlook of the other."

A year later, Dunlavey's analysis, in *The New Republic* of March 25, 1957, in which Skeffington is seen as an "Irish-American Machiavelli," would generally concur with West's viewpoint; but Dunlavey believed that West's charge of "genuinely subversive" seems to be "an overstrained effort at casual sensationalism." Dunlavey, who is aggravated by O'Connor's "irritating pretense of objectivity," claims that "the dimension of evil has been neatly excised." He argued that O'Connor has so manipulated that "every single indication of ruthlessness is carefully qualified to translate it into a shining evidence of virtue. It turns out, in every case, that Skeffington is really Doing Good" (16–17).

Anthony West's charge of "subversion" has occasioned two other responses in print by critics who are less willing to agree with his denunciation of the novel's moral turpitude. Thomas H. Eliot's review, "Robin Hood in Boston," which appeared in *The New Republic* of March 12, 1956, claimed that both the unqualified praise of some and West's attack have been "unduly intemperate." While Eliot agreed that Skeffington's encounters with evil are "unrealistic" and that Skeffington had been romanticized, Eliot withheld condemnation (28).

Schlesinger (p. 13), in suveying the controversy over the ethics of Skeffington, distinguished between the two major themes of the book and O'Connor's separate judgments about them: "The downfall of Skeffington and his brand of politics seemed to [O'Connor] inevitable, desirable and in the public interest. But he could not conceal his regret over the passing of gaudy and positive Irish personalities or over the disappearance of Irishness in the process of Americanization. Some critics, taking the second as the only judgment, misconstrued the book and denounced it as romantic, immoral and subversive." These critics, Schlesinger wrote, have accused O'Connor of placing a "sentimental gloss" over wicked times and evil men. But Schlesinger pointed out the difference between a valid observation and a political judgment.

Dunlavey's charge that Skeffington's characterization is "depthless" and that "nothing happens *inside* the man" must be rejected on the basis of the standard criteria used to evaluate characterization—description, analysis, speech, action, reactions of other characters. Certainly both the superlatives ("unforgettable character," etc.) used by critics and the resulting arguments about the ethics of Skeffington indicate that the weight of opinion also favors the view of Skeffington as a rather fully developed character. Howard Mumford Jones even suggested that Skeffington is "a character superbly seen and as intricate as any invention of Robert Browning."

Skeffington, as a man of action, is not prone to introspection, except for his deathbed reveries which reveal his very limitations. Part of Skeffington's tragedy is that he is "totally unaware" of why he lost the election, of what had happened to his tribe, and of how he was seen by others of a newer generation. Of these things, Skeffington is unaware; but O'Connor is not. If Skeffington's mentality is seen as oversimplistic, as mere maneuverings within a framework of assumed certitudes, then O'Connor is creating an appropriate and accurate reflection of a kind of man and of a type of society which did exist. Very few people in the "Catholic ghetto" world of Skeffington's heyday ever questioned the use of political clout for "good purposes" ("one of ours") or saw anything wrong with the "restitution" donations made by Catholic politicians, usurers, and gangsters to their local parish building fund.

Those who charge that Skeffington has been romanticized have a rather strong case within the boundaries of this novel. But just as it is legitimate to consider the wider ethical implications of Skeffington's actions, so also it is legitimate to consider the wider context, the real *milieu,* in which O'Connor wrote and in which *The Last Hurrah* was published. O'Connor's book was not (and is not) the first introduction to the "city boss" or "boss politics" which his reader is apt to have read. The terms "politician" and "city boss" have rather strong negative connotations suggesting images of ward-heelers, smoke-filled rooms, venal and corrupt men *à la* Nast's caricatures of Boss Tweed and Tammany Hall. Added to this view is the more modern concept of "government" as being an impersonal and unfeeling bureaucracy. Together, this cluster of pejorative images make up the dominant impression of local politics in modern society.

Considered in this context, *The Last Hurrah's* slanting can be seen as a reasonable counterbalance to a stereotype which also distorted the "reality" of boss politics by omitting its favorable aspects. O'Connor selectively emphasized three major factors, all of which had a solid basis in fact, for his version of the vanishing world of old-time politics: the humor of the eccentric politician, the benevolence of the informal welfare system, and the personal touch in politics. This era, O'Connor said, "was both wonderful and not fully understood, mostly misunderstood. . . . The young people nowadays lose sight of the fact that those old boys held people by personal loyalty alone. Now they are dying out, will not come back and belong to history."

Essentially, any argument over Skeffington's ethics probably reveals more about the critic's ideological position than about Skeffington. Skeffington, like Robin Hood, was a lawbreaker. Judged from a rigid legalistic position, these heroes are subversive. Judged, however, from a more relative viewpoint—either in terms of "situation ethics" or in terms of an *a priori* system which has many qualifications and exceptions built into its code—then an evaluation of Skeffington's actions becomes more complex. No easy answer is possible because one must consider not only the given situation within the novel, but the "real" situation that the fiction reflects. One cannot simply accept the "Robin Hood" concept that Skeffington stole from the rich WASP to give to the poor Irish. Immediately one thinks of the real evils and corruption of the city-hall politicos. Yet none of these real evils appears in *The Last Hurrah;* judged totally within the context of the situations presented in the novel, Skeffington may be considered a "good" man. Change of any part of this situation (add a murder, etc.) would necessitate a different evaluation; change any observer, and one would get a different evaluation. For example, Anthony West speaks approvingly of "the traditional New England Puritan ethics"; Irish immigrants had different feelings and terms for their WASP neighbors.

O'Connor has been charged with oversimplifying the issue, but he inserts, in three major sections of the book, a collection of arguments against Skeffington. By doing so, O'Connor has left the evaluation of Skeffington open-ended and has increased the richness of the novel; the reader, like Skeffington's nephew Adam Caufield, is left with the ambiguities of the situation. In O'Connor's later novel, *All in the Family* (1966), these ambiguities are continued as Jack and Charles discuss the merits of Skeffington (p. 180 ff.); again the contradictory positions are stated and the argument is left open-ended.

CHAPTER *6*

Benjy

I *Background*

IN September, 1956, a few months after the publication of *The Last Hurrah*, Edwin O'Connor's father died after years of illness; it is not known whether Doctor O'Connor, because of a lingering coma-like condition, ever comprehended his son's success. Following the funeral, as Schlesinger (p. 16) wrote, "Ed took his mother to Atlantic City for recuperation. There the sight of an odious little boy in the hotel stimulated him into beginning a cautionary story for children. This grew into the *jeu d'esprit* entitled *Benjy: A Ferocious Fairy Tale.*" O'Connor himself, in a *Newsweek* interview of October 21, 1957, related this story of the immediate stimulus for writing *Benjy* (118). Later, Mrs. Yntema, a senior editor at the Atlantic Monthly Press, recalled (in an interview with me) that as O'Connor neared the end of writing *Benjy,* he was searching for some kind of catastrophic ending, but had not yet decided on how to dispose of Benjy and his Mummy. In a conversation at a dinner party, Mrs. Yntema suggested the big bird; O'Connor picked up this idea from her and elaborated on it.

With such immediate authority for the origin of *Benjy,* it might seem unreasonable to suggest that *Benjy* may have deeper roots than that or be more than merely a *jeu d'esprit.* Nevertheless, any reader who attempts to understand the body of O'Connor's work should not bypass *Benjy.* Nor should *Benjy* and *I Was Dancing* be considered as mere "interludes" between O'Connor's three major novels. Serious attention should be given to these two lesser works, not so much for their intrinsic merit, as for their relation to the whole.

In the context of most other "children's stories," *Benjy* is unusual and atypical, but several of the offbeat qualities of the book seem derivative from other sources. The cigar-smoking Good Fairy, for example, seems to be a direct borrowing from the cigar-smoking Mr. O'Malley, the Fairy Godfather of Crockett Johnson's comic strip, "Barnaby." Nor is the offbeat ending of a "fairy tale" original to O'Connor. In 1953, for example, Steve Allen's *Grimm Fairy Tales for Hip Kids,* read by Al "Jazzbo" Collins, was a best-selling record that encouraged a fad of "updating" traditional fairy tales with modern slang, puns, and offbeat episodes. Since then, such whimsy has been prominent in several television cartoon series, including "Bullwinkle," which O'Connor enjoyed watching.

The text of *Benjy,* which runs approximately seventeen thousand words, is accompanied by thirty imaginative illustrations by Ati Forberg; the overall design, layout, and typography of the volume is strikingly handsome. Yet, as Mrs. Yntema noted, in *The Best and the Last of Edwin O'Connor* (p. 151): "*Benjy* gained a handful of devoted admirers, mostly children, but had no popular success and is now out of print." One reason for its limited publishing history is that *Benjy* is not the type of book which educators and librarians could (or would) put on a standard "reading list." Because of the ironic style, which uses the very same clichés of didactic children's literature and mocks the very "virtues" (being good to Mommy, helping teacher) seriously preached in many books, *Benjy* is not the kind of book to be recommended to every young reader. Older children (in the middle grades) are apt to understand the satire in light of their previous reading experience, but younger children are more apt to focus on the incongruities of situation. If read aloud to children, the book must be pre-read first in order for the reader to catch the appropriate voice tones and the sarcasm necessary to differentiate some sections of it from the ordinary didactic story. (My own children enjoyed *Benjy,* and have offered their considered opinions of it: Elizabeth (9) felt that "Benjy is a spoiled child whose mother is very proud of her diploma"; Christopher (8) thought Benjy was "a finky little kid" with a "nutty mother"; James-Jonathan (6) felt strong empathy for the Dirty Boy, "the guy who punched Benjy in the eye"; David (5) most enjoyed Sid catching flies and Daddy in the TV set, although he too felt that Benjy was "silly.")

II *The Story*

In the true fairy-tale fashion, O'Connor begins the story of Benjy and his Mummy: "Once upon a time, not so many years ago, there lived in a small town called Smiles, Pennsylvania, a little boy named Benjamin Thurlow Ballou. He had no brothers and no sisters. He lived all alone with his mother, his father, and his doggie. His mother who was a college graduate, was named Mummy. His father, who was a television repairman, was named Daddy. And his doggie, who was an Airedale, was named Sid. They all lived together in a nice little house, and they were very happy there." In the first chapter, Mummy and Daddy are discussing what nickname to use for their only child, now one year old. Daddy, who is crouched inside his television set, playing solitaire and eating a sandwich, suggests "George," only to be overruled by Mummy, who decides on "Benjy." After admiring her framed college diploma and commenting on "others around here who haven't had my advantages," Mummy goes upstairs to Benjy's bedroom to cover him with kisses. Meanwhile, Sid, who has been catching flies—"an Airedale's way of having fun," is busy counting his catch.

The second chapter shows Benjy, at three years old, playing his cute games: kissing and hugging and snuggling with Mommy, evicting Daddy from bed, and causing Sid to be exiled to a box in the back yard. The next three chapters describe Benjy's first day at school. After Mummy dresses Benjy in his new fudge-colored velvet suit, she puts on her cap and gown, and they skip along to school together "laughing and playing games like 'Pease Porridge Hot', and singing her school song." Once inside the school, Benjy must be left alone; so Mummy contents herself with bobbing up and down at the window playing Peekaboo, until Miss Teacher and Mister Principal call Mister School Policeman who goes out to speak to Mummy.

The following two chapters show Benjy the Busy Beaver in action at school where he is the very best little pupil in class: he does all his lessons, he knows all the answers, he sings the loudest, he helps the teacher, and, in all of his spare time, he recites "the Pledge of Allegiance" because he is so proud to be an American. Benjy's scholastic efforts are rewarded when a Dirty Little Boy puts his Dirty Little Fist into Benjy's baby-blue eye. Mummy's frantic reaction is directed against the Principal, the Police Chief, the Mayor, and Daddy. Afterwards, Benjy quits playing with the naughty first-grade boys; he plays instead with the nice little girls.

One day on the way home from school, a Good Fairy appears to Benjy. Instead of a pretty lady with lovely robes, Benjy's Good Fairy is a big fat man with little eyes and a big red bulby nose. Wearing a baseball suit, smoking a cigar, and coughing, he speaks like a Damon Runyan character: "Whaddaya say, kid? I'm ya Good Fairy!" After batting fungoes for a while, the Good Fairy gets down to business and asks Benjy what is his *wish*: "Howja like ta be a big athalete some day? . . . Howsa bout becomin' a fighter? Heavyweight champeen o' the world, maybe?" Benjy responds with a few pious wishes which the Good Fairy rejects as being too vague. Then Benjy, thinking always of his Mummy, wishes "that whatever big and marvelous things happen to little Benjy, the very same big and marvelous things will happen to his dear Mummy, too!" The Good Fairy leaves, requiring Benjy to remain silent about the visit.

Life at the Ballou household continues as usual: Benjy behaves as a good boy should, Mummy knits a lovely pink sweater for him, Daddy plays cards inside the TV set. One night, just as Benjy is about to reveal the big secret, the smell of cigar smoke permeates the house; and Benjy's revelation is stopped by Mummy's furious tirade against her nicotine-fiend husband; but Daddy isn't smoking at all. In the final chapter, the family goes to the Picnic Place on Mount Laugh for their annual Daddy's Birthday Picnic, an event pleasing to Mummy because Daddy doesn't like picnics. After the meal, Benjy discovers a huge bird's nest with a huge egg in it. Mummy says it's an *"abandoned* eggie" left by "very bad Mummy birds who don't love their little eggies." Benjy goes to take the egg; Daddy's warning to him not to touch it infuriates Mummy. Benjy drops the egg, splattering it. From the sky, with a noise like a huge jet, an enormous black Mummy Bird swoops down and carries off Benjy. An instant later, a huge Daddy Bird picks up Mummy, and the birds disappear with their catch. The Good Fairy, who had been watching all of this, scratches Benjy's name off his list now that Benjy's wish has been granted.

Daddy and Sid return to the house to watch television. Instead of crouching inside the set, Daddy sits in the best chair, with his feet on another, opens a can of beer, and Sid stretches out on Mummy's favorite pillow with his muddy paws on the rug. As they watch television, the news announcer (akin to Christopher Usher's gushing, human-interest stories in *The Oracle*) tells of the tragedy; after the news, Daddy turns on a Western, drinks his beer, lights a good cigar, and occasionally wonders about Mummy and Benjy. The story ends: "On the whole, he thought, it was very possible that they would never come back. And they never did."

III *Critical Response*

While reviewers for the mass-circulation magazines generally enjoyed *Benjy* but had some puzzled reservations, the reviewers for journals directed at librarians and professional educators were rather violent in their attacks on the book. The *Kirkus* review of August 15, 1957, for example, said: "Just what purpose is served by this tale—unless Edwin O'Connor is getting back at someone —remains a mystery. Seek as one does for symbolism, humor, any *raison d'être* one reaches the end mystified as to why the story was written, for whom it is intended, and why it is being published" (593). The *Library Journal* of September 15, 1957, termed it "heavy-handed," written "in a sort of leering baby-talk," and advised that "Mr. O'Connor had better stick to politicians" (2141).

On the other hand, the *Time* review of October 21, 1957 called it a "blithe-spirited Thurberesque fable" noting that "Though the fun sometimes wears thin, *Benjy* is a striking display of virtuosity, proving that its author can move with literary ease from Curley to curlylocks" (108). Martin Levin, in *Saturday Review* of December 14, 1957, saw it as a "shaggy dog parable" and a "rabbit punch at Mom . . . evidently gotten up for the holiday trade—and a refreshing change it is from the usual seasonal sugarplum" (15). David Dempsey, in the *New York Times* of October 20, 1957, also noted its seasonal timing: "Readers will enjoy *Benjy* if they like their whimsy sophisticated . . . an excellent Christmas gift. Just don't give it to Mom" (4). *Newsweek* of October 21, 1957, in a review which accompanies the interview with O'Connor, concluded: "It seems clear that smart children reading *Benjy* will get a fine fairy-tale indoctrination against Momism, and that grownups who are not too fervidly matriarchal will enjoy the trifle themselves" (118).

Two reviewers especially pointed out the ambiguities they sensed in the book. Robert Healey, in the *New York Herald Tribune* of November 3, 1957, called *Benjy* a "curious literary finger exercise" and wondered that it "may be a mordant parody of cloying children's books or perhaps a protest against cloying children. Then again it may be a sardonic attack on momism, or mummyism, as we should call it here. The initial premise is amusing, but the development is archly coy and the conscious treacle of the style runs very thin in the course of the little volume" (12). William Hogan, in the *San Francisco Chronicle* (October 15, 1957), labeled *Benjy* as the "most offbeat book" of the year and commented: "I don't suppose Edwin O'Connor hates children so much as he hates doting mothers. Perhaps it is the nasty-nice juvenile book he hates. He must hate something, because *Benjy*, this ferocious fairy tale, as he calls it, is the most devastating satire I have yet seen on 'Good Little Boys', on overly protective mothers and some brands of overly saccharine books for children." After summarizing the story, Hogan concludes his review: "So in this ferocious fairy tale we perhaps read The Secret Life of Edwin O'Connor, in its way as eminently satisfying a story as anything told by The Brothers Grimm. What does it mean? If he knows, O'Connor isn't telling. So far as I know, the secret might be pried out only by a good Viennese Specialist" (25).

Schlesinger (p. 17) refrained from extensive comment on *Benjy* other than to relate its "origin" at the Atlantic City hotel, describe its basic story, and term it an "ambiguous little volume." Calling it a "black comedy," he noted the exceedingly mixed reaction to the book: "Tenderhearted adults were repelled by what they considered the violence of the underlying fantasy; tougher readers were delighted by the satire. Children, less given to weighing psychological implications, seem to have relished it."

Edmund Wilson, in the final paragraph of the "Baldini" memoir, offered his own analysis of O'Connor's motive for writing *Benjy*. Wilson, who praised O'Connor's personal virtues, saw *Benjy* as a deliberate self-mockery: "I believe that the explanation of his satirical children's fable *Benjy*—the story of a horrid little prig who makes trouble for everyone else—is that Ed was always on his guard about letting people be conscious of his virtuous habits because he realized how easy it would be for these to become obnoxious. He neither smoked nor drank; he was considerate and incorruptible."

CHAPTER 7

The Edge of Sadness

I Background

AFTER the success of *The Last Hurrah*, certain aspects of O'Connor's style of living changed noticeably, yet he remained within the environment he had so long enjoyed. For a decade, O'Connor had been the impoverished writer earning a bare living in small rented rooms, walking and bicycling through the streets of downtown Boston, vacationing at an old cabin at Cape Cod, and enjoying a social life usually as a guest at friends' parties. When the money from *The Last Hurrah*—the prize money, the royalties, the book-club fees—suddenly arrived, O'Connor left his rooming house and moved to an apartment on Beacon Street on the edge of Boston Common; coincidently, he was located directly across from the monument erected by Mayor Curley. Later, he rented a house on Chestnut Street and furnished it with museum-piece Italian Renaissance furniture before he eventually bought a mansion on Marlborough Street, directly across the street from where he had originally lived in the rooming house. To supplement his bicycle, O'Connor bought a car. To keep his Cape Cod excursions, he built an architect-designed summer home there. To continue his social life, O'Connor now functioned as host, frequently giving parties for his old circle of friends. In addition, he also became the source of loans, frequently unrepaid, to a host of acquaintances with hard-luck stories.

While this sudden influx of money did have an effect on O'Connor, he did not seem to lose his equilibrium. Later, in the first part of *All in the Family* as Jack's father speaks about money, one can sense that this is O'Connor himself working out a personal credo about the proper use of money as a means, not an end, in life. Generally speaking, O'Connor's spending was modest and restricted, if one considers a dozen other options available to him; but the "good life," for him, was in Boston among his friends. Schlesinger (p. 16) recalled that his affluence amused O'Connor: "Except for an addiction to foreign cars, he spent very little on himself. His Beacon Hill apartment had an almost monastic air, especially in the cell-like bedroom where a simple crucifix hung above what can only be described as a pallet. He wore the same terrycloth jacket to the beach for years despite the protest and derision of friends, and his hat, when he put one on, was disreputable in the extreme."

More important is what O'Connor did with his time. After *The Last Hurrah* made him famous, he was besieged by offers to lecture, to appear on television shows, and to write for magazines; but he rejected all of them. The only "extra" writing he did in this period was a series of articles, donated free to the *Boston Post*, in an effort to help save that newspaper which had once sustained him and on which many of his journalist friends depended. Thus, instead of living a life of luxury or hacking out articles and books to capitalize on his literary fame, O'Connor used the security and leisure afforded him by his new money to concentrate on his fiction. During the five years following *The Last Hurrah*, O'Connor published very little (the brief *Benjy*, the *Boston Post* articles) and lectured very rarely (at the Paulist Center in Boston; at Frank O'Malley's classes at Notre Dame). During this period, O'Connor's attention was focused on his novel-in-progress, *The Edge of Sadness*, and on the rigorous stylistic demands he was setting for himself in telling this subtle, complex story about a priest.

O'Connor had known many priests during his life, both at Notre Dame and in the Boston area. At one time, during his youth, he had even considered becoming a priest. Though he chose not to be one, he remained very sympathetic and aware of the life and the problems of the clergy. Moreover, his religious life was important to him; he commonly went to mass and communion during the week. Edmund Wilson, in the "Baldini" memoir, saw O'Connor as "one of the few educated friends I have had who struck me as sincerely attempting to lead the life of a Christian." As a bachelor, intensely interested in religion, the church, and the clergy, O'Connor had a special affinity with priests and was a welcomed guest and companion of many of the Catholic clergy in Boston.

II *The Novel*

The Edge of Sadness opens with the narrator, Father Hugh Kennedy, disclaiming that the narrative is *his* story; it will be a story about the Carmody family, a family dominated by the gruff old patriarch, Charlie Carmody. This narrative device can be misleading, for many reviewers accepted Father Hugh's statement at face value. But, if the reader recognizes the extreme importance of any first-person narrator, he will appreciate the skill of this feint: the priest's own story will be revealed in his narration. After the disclaimer, Father Hugh introduces the basic situation and the relevant background material. He is now fifty-five years old, thirty years a priest, and the pastor of a parish in a rundown part of the city.

An early morning telephone call from Charlie Carmody revives memories of former days when Charlie had been a "friend" of Hugh's father and when Hugh had been a friend of Charlie's son, John, at the seminary. The intricate father-son relationship, which dominates this novel, begins in such a low-keyed manner that it is only in the re-reading of the novel that one can fully appreciate the amount of characterization being presented by these early, apparently random, fragments. By the end of the first chapter, two foreshadowings have also been quietly introduced as Father Hugh wonders about Charlie's motive for inviting him to a forthcoming birthday party, a family reunion affair: "I knew at once that Charlie wanted something, that he wanted it badly, and that he wanted it from me. But exactly what he could want—or, for that matter, what I had to give—was beyond me." In addition, the reader is apt to wonder about "all that had happened" in Father Hugh's past, events which seem to have been painful to him.

The second chapter takes place on the Sunday of Charlie Carmody's birthday party, a Sunday which is, ironically, the feast of Saint Paul, the Apostle of Charity, the patron saint of Father Hugh's parish. The chapter begins with Father Hugh's meditations about the changes within the Catholic Church as he thinks about the old-time sermons in contrast to the new and about the old-time pastors who received an "exasperated idolatry" from a homogeneous laity in contrast to the newer pastors and newer laity. O'Connor weaves a great deal of informed sociological commentary into these meditations, but the main emphasis of the

chapter is on two priests, Father Danowski and Father John
Carmody, who act throughout the novel as foil characters to
Father Hugh.

Father Danowski, Father Hugh's curate-assistant at Old Saint
Paul's, is, despite his youth, actually a representative of an older
generation. Coming from immigrant Polish stock, a much later
immigrant group than the Irish, Father Danowski not only has
many of the common characteristics of the ghetto mentality, but
also is characterized by a pretentious, old-fashioned rhetoric
which underlines his ties to the past. Father Danowski is honest,
zealous, holy, sincere; but he is also naïve, provincial, humorless,
and, sometimes, stupid. He had entered the seminary at an early
age, plodded through his studies with more endurance than intelligence, and, in the action of the story, works zealously in the
old parish blithely dreaming of a "bigger and better" parish. He
equates "success" with measurable gains; and he admires a
Father Cassidy, his former classmate, who now performs on television as the "Whistling Priest" and reaches "those who might
otherwise be missed" by sandwiching a whistled "Ave Maria" in
between "How Much is that Doggie in the Window?" and the
sponsor's commercial. Father Hugh's reaction to his curate, here
and generally throughout the novel, is primarily a mixture of
amusement and disdain.

In contrast to Father Danowski's shallow optimism, Father
John Carmody is presented as a cynical and sardonic misan-
thrope; embittered, dissatisfied with everyone and everything,
and, exasperated with the whining complaints of his parishioners,
he is especially antagonistic toward his own father, Charlie Carmody. A full characterization of Father John is not presented in
this chapter because O'Connor uses the method of revealing
character obliquely through fragments and indirections, but the
reader should be alert to these two foil characters and to the
important father-son theme which is emphasized in this early
chapter.

Here, Father Hugh relates, "I had never met Father Danowski's father, but it made no difference; by now he had emerged
from our conversations as a vivid figure, larger than life . . . a man
of great strength and independent spirit" forever creating maxims
which Father Danowski memorized and frequently retold. Later,
when Father Hugh actually meets the old man, the narrator is

surprised to find that Father Danowski's father is a small man, extremely shy and silent: "far from being the firebrand of his son's stories, he seemed a mild and even a submissive man." But the filial adoration of this naïve curate interprets such silence in this meeting as a proof of his father's great reverence for the priesthood—as a difficult restraint for the old man who could "overwhelm" a person with his power of words. In the novel, Father Danowski's simple loyalty and love for his father help to highlight the malice and spite of Father Carmody's reaction to his father.

Father John Carmody's attitude toward his father, Charlie, is one of suspicion, bitterness, and hostility that developed from a "fitful exasperation" during John's seminary days to a "far more grievous" attitude by the end of his life. His "vexation had hardened into something else," perhaps sheer hatred. This obsession of Father Carmody is based not only on what Charlie had done to him, but also on how Charlie had wrecked the lives of all within the Carmody family. Charlie's tyrannical influence is seen by John, later in the novel, as being so powerful that even he, himself, doubts his own motives for entering the priesthood.

The brief (5 pp.) third chapter, in which Father Hugh and Father John Carmody arrive at Charlie Carmody's house, provides a detailed description of the Victorian gingerbread mansion, adds to the characterization of Charlie as an egocentric self-styled patriarch, and gives the first specific clue as to Father Hugh's problem in the past. Charlie welcomes Father Hugh with a cheerful greeting, "It's grand to see you. . . . It's been a long time between drinks, as the poet says." Father Hugh immediately relates: "He had no sooner said this than a slight but curious change came over his face. I had the extraordinary feeling that I was caught up in a rare moment, that I was seeing Charlie actually embarrassed. Did he suspect that his convivial poet's phrase had a peculiar inappropriateness when addressed to me?"

After the third chapter, the surface action of the novel becomes more complicated because the whole Carmody clan is introduced in the fourth chapter; but, before this family reunion scene opens, O'Connor has already established the direction of the novel. In the foreground, propelling the reader's interest, are the anticipated revelations: one expects Charlie's motives and Father Hugh's alcoholism to be revealed. In the background, less noticeable because of their fragment form, are the major themes of the father-son relationships and of Father Hugh's inner conflict. If these major patterns are discerned, then the many complications (additional characters, anecdotal material, etc.) can be regarded as the delicate counterpointing that they are, instead of as a mere accumulation of Irish-American local color.

Structurally, the novel is centered upon a few scenes rendered in depth. The birthday party, the rectory, the flashback to the Cenacle rest home, and the wake constitute the bulk of the novel. O'Connor's basic technique is the use of a dialogue between the narrator and one other character. Even in crowd scenes, there are seldom any conversations in which more than two people are talking. O'Connor focuses sharply on one character for several pages, then, using the narrator's analysis as a transition, shifts to another character. In spite of the crowded stage, the reader never gets lost because of this narrative device.

In Chapter Four, fifteen people, representing four generations, are assembled in the living room for Charlie's party. The eldest members, who are in their eighties, are Charlie's contemporaries: his widowed sister, Julia; his maid, Agnes; and his cronies, Bucky Heffernan and P.J. Mulcahy. The next generation is that of Father Hugh and of Charlie's children, all in their fifties: Father John Carmody, Mary Carmody, Dan Carmody and his wife Flo, Helen Carmody O'Donnell and her husband, Doctor Frank O'Donnell. Helen's son, Ted O'Donnell, and his wife, Anne, are in their late twenties; and they have their three-year-old twins with them. After the introduction scene, there are four brief scenes as Father Hugh makes his way across the room and talks with the various family members.

As he talks with Helen, he becomes increasingly aware that they have all aged; he remembers her from her youth and finds it strange to see her as a grandmother. The scene with Mary allows Father John to make some sarcastic comments about his father, who has exploited Mary's docile simplicity. When Father Hugh talks with the two old cronies, Bucky probes about Father Hugh's long absence in the West, while P.J. kindly tries to divert this conversation. Finally, Doctor Frank O'Donnell, a patronizing bore, congratulates Father Hugh. In these last two scenes, the reader becomes aware of the borderline between shame and embarrassment that Father Hugh is walking as he makes his long delayed re-entry into a society in which he had once functioned freely.

Chapter Five continues the birthday party, but the focus now shifts to Charlie Carmody. Seated next to the young Anne O'Donnell, Father Hugh learns about Ted's political ambitions as an A.D.A. liberal Democrat who plans to run for Congress. What shocks the priest is that Ted and Anne haven't even informed Charlie of these plans: "the old man with the iron hand over all his family did not even enter the lives of his grandchildren!" P.J. and Bucky interrupt with their reminiscences about the eccentric characters of the "good old days" at Saint Paul's before it began to be "run down." After these two preludes that emphasize the changing generations Charlie Carmody begins dominating the table talk.

Charlie's monologue, which extends for nearly ten pages, is a meticulously constructed aria; the sequence of ideas defies logic, but the authenticity of this speech pattern can be testified to by those who have experienced the rituals of a family reunion. His egocentric speech rambles wildly through anecdotes about illnesses and dead friends, through the zany interruptions of his cronies, who also want to get into the act; but it always returns to praise or to pity Charlie Carmody. Everything he says reveals some aspect of himself as being sardonically witty, abusively humorous, mean-spirited, cantankerous, and self-centered. Furthermore, O'Connor inserts several major themes as Charlie teases Father John, hints about Father Hugh's past, and closes by reminding Father Hugh about an intended "little chat."

After Charlie leaves the room, the focus shifts back to Father Hugh. He says goodbye to various people, but the emphasis is on his talk with Helen. Here again, as in the initial dialogue framing this chapter, Father Hugh is nostalgic as he speaks with her. Although he thinks that she, of all the Carmodys, has come closest to satisfaction and contentment in life, he detects a "queer touch of sadness" in her voice as they speak.

The Sixth Chapter, which closes Book I, is proportionately as long as the first five chapters together, running nearly seventy pages. The chapter opens as Father Carmody is leaving the party; he and Father Hugh compare notes about their priestly duties and about Charlie. Father John describes his busy daily routine as the pastor of the "successful" Saint Raymond's parish. He dislikes his job and the constant contact with people; ironically, he yearns for the solitude which Father Hugh has in his dull parish. As Father John criticizes Charlie's long-winded speech, one can sense O'Connor's attention to craft in trying to reproduce the "detour" style of Charlie's rambling talk: "In all rational talk," says Father John, "no matter how much you digress, you usually come back to the main road once in a while. But in my father's house no one comes back to the main road for the simple reason that there *is* no main road. Everybody there deals exclusively in detours."

Returning to the rectory, Father Hugh briefly meets the exuberant Father Danowski whose cheerful attitudes are juxtaposed to Father John's cynicism. Father Hugh then retires to his room where he has a long solitary meditation about his parish and the slum neighborhood, about the false images of a priest (noted later in this study in Section III), about his own inactivity, and about death. These somber contemplative analyses by Father Hugh, which comprise a good portion of the book, are *necessary* to develop the introspective character of the narrator and are *readable* not only because of the quality of the insights but also because of the concreteness of the style. O'Connor, in dealing with some evasive abstractions, is careful to work with vivid concrete details.

Interrupted by a phone call, Father Hugh is summoned to the "deathbed" of a Mrs. Sanchez, a pietistic old woman whose sinless confession reveals her self-satisfied smugness in her religion. This scene foreshadows Charlie's deathbed scene, and it also makes Father Hugh think about the varieties of religious experience. Mrs. Sanchez's attitude reminds the narrator of the complacent certitude of the stern old authoritarian Archbishop Garland. After this reminder, Father Hugh thinks about another distasteful religious attitude as he overhears an evangelical radio broadcast in which a businessman is delivering an "inspirational" sermon on brotherhood. At such times, Father Hugh feels that the gap between him and his people is "miles wide and unmeasureably deep"; he returns to his room to take consolation in reading his favorite religious writer, Cardinal Newman.

Unable to concentrate on his reading, Father Hugh begins to think about those events in his past which have led him to this present situation. This long reverie extends for nearly forty pages, but it is divided into six major sections in chronological order, thereby providing a strong framework for these fragments of memory. At first, Father Hugh recalls his happy days as a young priest, zealous and busy, for fifteen years as a curate at Saint Raymond's and for five years as a pastor at Saint Stephen's. Here, the description of his priestly duties, especially of the many non-sacramental jobs of the parish priest, corresponds accurately to the dominant image of the American Catholic clergy of this era.

Then Father Hugh shifts his narrative to tell about the sickness and death of his own father, Dave Kennedy. When his widowed father got cancer, Father Hugh felt impotent to help and endured a long, agonizing period as he witnessed the old man die: "Every day and every night I had prayed that he might be allowed either the miracle of recovery or the blessing of a happy death. These prayers were not answered. My father did not recover, and he died witless and in pain." The effect of this death agony on Father Hugh is traumatic; although his attempt to reconcile "pain and suffering with an omnipotent and merciful God" does not cause him to lose his faith, it causes a radical change in his behavior.

With this story of his father's death as a prelude, Father Hugh reveals his subsequent problem as he begins to drink heavily and to withdraw into a sullen isolation. In this period of ennui, characterized not so much by bitterness as by a sheer lack of concern for anyone or anything, Father Hugh analyzes his previous life as a priest and concludes that he has spent his life in busywork, "a cheerleader in a Roman collar."

Summoned for counseling by the bishop, a kind, understanding man, Father Hugh stops drinking for two months; then he suddenly relapses, during a period of depression, into hard drinking. Sent by the bishop to the Cenacle, a rest home for alcoholic priests in the Arizona desert, Father Hugh spends the next four years with a group of twenty other priests. The only character among them who is described in detail is a gregarious priest, with winning personal charms, who acts as a foil to Father Hugh. Despite all the good qualities of this friendly priest. Father Hugh recognizes that the man is not honest with himself, avoids the reality of his own alcoholism, and continually creates alibis and illusions about his backsliding.

Finally, Father Hugh is returned to his priestly duties and assigned as pastor of Saint Paul's, apparently a haven for misfits and failures as he describes his encounters with Roy, the crazy janitor (akin to the janitor in "Parish Reunion"), and Father Danowski, his absurd curate. Coming out of this long reverie, Father Hugh is thinking of his present situation when Charlie Carmody's telephone call interrupts him. Charlie rambles on, seemingly without purpose, and hangs up before Father Hugh can pin him down as to why he called. With this sub-plot reintroduced here, Book I ends with Father Hugh wondering about Charlie's motives in trying to establish a friendship with him now.

In Book II, which is comprised of chapters Seven and Eight, Chapter Seven opens in the "interval of quiet" away from Father Hugh's concern with the Carmody family. After extensive preparation at Saint Paul's, the anticipated visit by the bishop finally takes place, allowing Father Hugh an opportunity to talk with his kind superior. Despite his conscious acceptance of his job at Saint Paul's, Father Hugh suddenly finds himself excited about the possibility of getting out, of being promoted to a "better" parish: "that crazy surge of delighted anticipation for something I'd convinced myself I no longer wanted—came to me often and disquietingly, reminding me that we are seldom as fixed and sure as we believe ourselves to be. Sometimes just a puff of temptation, and the backbone cracks. . . ." This vital foreshadowing of Father Hugh's ultimate decision is then followed by a series of scenes which emphasize the false illusions and self-delusions of others in the story.

Father Hugh meets Father Danowski's legendary father only to find him a far cry from his son's version of him. Daniel Carmody, the "black sheep" failure of the family, who sees himself as a super-salesman, visits Father Hugh to try to sell him stock in his latest venture. Then Charlie Carmody stops by the rectory, toys with Father Danowski, who has illusions about getting a big donation from Charlie for the parish, and then invites Father Hugh to accompany him to the hospital to visit Bucky. At the hospital, Bucky is watching television (giving O'Connor a chance to satirize several phony programs), but soon Charlie dominates the scene by telling stories to Bucky about Dave Kennedy. Father Hugh realizes that these are pure fantasy inventions and is amazed at the "preposterous performance" he witnesses.

Chapter Eight takes place, months later, in autumn, as Father

Hugh is concerned with his parish duties; Charlie Carmody had been stopping by every ten days or so in the interim, but the purpose of his visits remain a mystery to Father Hugh. A conversation with Father John shows Father Hugh's admiration for the other priest's sense of liturgy, a reverent and esthetic appreciation of the forms of worship in contrast to the mechanical routine of many priests; but their talk also covers family matters and shows Father John's continuing antagonism toward his father. Bucky Heffernan also visits the rectory, trying to enlist Father Hugh in his almost-conspiratorial plan that the old man has about his own funeral and gravestone, an obsession which dramatizes his egocentric illusions.

However, the major scene in this chapter is the extended rendering of Helen's visit to Father Hugh in which their talk covers a good portion of the Carmody clan. Minor characters are more fully developed here (Frank as insensitive husband, Dan as drifter, and so on) and the complex inter-relationships within generations of the family are suggested. Father Hugh is also able, for the first time, to talk about his own problem; and he tells his "whole story" to Helen. O'Connor does not repeat the previously told details here, but fills in with Father Hugh's story of his parishioners' reaction to his alcoholism. After Father Hugh concludes, he feels ashamed that he has said so much "merely out of some ludicrous, little-boy desire to feel a soothing hand on the brow," perhaps underlining the maternal image which Helen seems to suggest. Helen is sympathetic, but she reasonably encourages him to avoid self-pity and to recognize that most other adults also have problems.

Following this talk with a perceptive intimate who has no illusions, the next scene focuses on Father Danowski with his absurd speculations about the invention of Jello. Again, O'Connor has juxtaposed a realist (Helen) between two dreamers (Bucky and Father Danowski), but Father Hugh's reaction to Father Danowski is more complex and ambiguous as the narrator realizes that the curate, with all of his drawbacks, is admirably zealous in trying to do his job as a priest. Perhaps this is another of the "shattering dualities" which Father Hugh spoke about to Helen. Father Hugh retires alone to the church to pray, but he is unable to concentrate. Returning to his room, he receives another call from Charlie Carmody, mystifying in its vagueness; and the chap-

ter (and Book II) closes on this same suspense device used at
the end of Book I.

Chapters Nine and Ten (Book III) occur at Christmas. Chapter Nine begins as Father Hugh relates his discouragement about
the apathy of his parishioners during that season. But the enthusiastic Father Danowski, unaware of the realities of the situation,
is making elaborate plans and preparations at the church. Most
of the chapter centers on Father Danowski and his "astonishing
mannerisms," from the archaic pomposity of his sermon style to
his unmitigated admiration for the "Whistling Priest." The curate's youth, seminary days, and sense of vocation are all described by Father Hugh, who recognizes the shallowness of the
naïve young priest. After talking with Father Danowski, Father
Hugh goes to the empty church to meditate and becomes extremely depressed, perhaps as a result of this double dose of his
parishioners' apathy and his curate's zeal. Alone at the rectory,
Father Hugh's melancholy deepens to a sense of sadness and
hopelessness. Again the phone interrupts his thoughts, and the
chapter closes with Charlie Carmody's sister urgently asking the
priest to come to the house because Charlie has collapsed and
appears to be dying.

Chapter Ten opens as Father Hugh, at the Carmody house,
talks with Doctor Frank O'Donnell. Previously the priest had
considered Frank a phony and a bore, but now Frank reveals
some genuine qualities, albeit one is his total indifference to his
father-in-law's probable death. Other family members and friends
begin arriving as another gathering of the clan, parallel to the
earlier party scene, takes place at Charlie's request. Father John,
as usual, is cynical about the tableau which Charlie wants to
stage, and he dubs his father "the Belasco of the invalids." As
they all wait outside Charlie's room for the Francisan priest
within to finish hearing Charlie's confession, Bucky and P.J. argue
over inanities; and the young Ted reveals his crass unfeeling attitudes, ones far distant from the older generation. This revelation
prompts Father Hugh to defend Charlie for being a real person,
at least, instead of a mere cipher.

After the Franciscan leaves, Charlie asks to see Father Hugh
alone. Exchanging humorous pleasantries at first, the two men
then begin talking about death. Here, for the first time, Charlie
speaks with great integrity, "without a mask of any kind," with-

out self-pity or sentimentality as he rages against his anticipated death and says that he "won't be missed." Speaking flatly, Charlie states: "I'll tell you somethin' I never told you or anybody else before. And that is that everythin' I told you about me bein' so popular and havin' a lot of friends and people wantin' to be like me is all bunk. It ain't true. . . . there's not a man in the city today that's more hated than me." Father Hugh finds it hard to listen to this emotionless self-analysis coming from Charlie with such conviction. "Stripped of all hypocrisy or falseness, it was impossible to dismiss or discount; listening to him I had only the impression of a terrible sincerity."

Charlie explains his lifelong dilemma: in order to succeed in his climb out of the tough ghetto conditions of his youth, he had to be tough; but this sternness had cost him dearly. Desolately, he recounts his children's attitudes toward him: Mary is docile and simple-minded; Dan is shallow and stupid; John is "cold as an icicle"; Helen hates him (an unexpected remark which prompts Charlie to a fuller explanation, a story of Helen's youthful outburst). Speaking of other family members and friends, Charlie shares Father Hugh's opinion about young Ted's callousness; and he concludes by pointing out that his old cronies, Bucky and P.J., are too egocentric to really care about him: "old men don't miss nobody. When you're old and someone else that's old dies you might say out loud, 'Ain't that a shame!' but what you say to yourself is, 'One more gone, and the next one might be me'."

After this long lament, Father Hugh attempts to console Charlie by reminding him of the temptations of despair and lack of charity. But Charlie affirms his faith in God; in fact, what he wants is a "special break" from God. What Charlie wants from Father Hugh, however, after an oblique approach to the subject, is Father Hugh's assurance that *his* father, Dave Kennedy, really loved Charlie: "The mystery was solved. The great game of What-Was-Charlie-Up-To was over, and all my speculations and suspicions—and John's as well—had been ingenious, shrewdly reasoned, and completely wrong. For what Charlie had been up to all along was nothing more than . . . a pat on the back from my dead father. Passed on by the one possible middleman."

The situation is unbearably pathetic to the priest; out of compassion for Charlie, Father Hugh lies, telling the old man about

Dave Kennedy's "great affection" for him and illustrating it with anecdotes from the good old days. With affection and pity, Father Hugh fabricates a story for the apparently dying man. Afterwards, Charlie, without any of the expected amenities, brusquely dismisses the priest. Father Hugh talks briefly with the family waiting outside before he returns to the rectory.

Chapter Eleven (and Book IV) takes place in the subsequent "waiting period" that week. Because of Charlie's condition and because of the death of an old vagrant, found in an aisle of the church, the hint of death permeates the rectory despite Father Danowski's attempts to cheer Father Hugh. Ted fulfills a promised visit to Father Hugh, offering to be an usher at the church, a calculated move designed to win votes in the district. Father Hugh rejects this cynical proposition, using the story of Jigger Toomey, an old-time political hack, as an *exemplum* of such crass manipulation in the past. Afterwards, Father Hugh goes to the Carmody house to visit Charlie, but the old man is sleeping. The priest talks briefly with the ne'er-do-well Dan, listening to his fantasies, before going to Saint Raymond's to visit Father John, in what is the climactic scene of the novel. The question of Charlie's motives for seeking Hugh's friendship was resolved in the "deathbed" scene, causing some critics who had been focusing on Charlie to complain of the long anticlimactic section following the resolution of this mystery. But what happens is that, with this suspense removed, the center of attention shifts to Father Kennedy's priestly life; and the novel reaches its climax in the bitter invectives of Father John Carmody's denunciation of Father Kennedy's lethargy and egocentricity.

As Father Hugh arrives at Saint Raymond's, he grows nostalgic because this parish is so meaningful to his past life; in contrast, he is greeted by Father John whose sardonic humor about the parish activities reflects his bitterness and disgust. Father John, almost in a monologue, dominates the conversation as he begins to speak of his own unhappy youth in a vicious complaint against the damage caused by his tyrannical father to all of the Carmody children. After this subject, Father John switches to an exasperated diatribe against his parishioners' whining demands on him— a misanthropic outburst of hostility towards his people that borders on the verge of hysteria. When Father Hugh tries to calm him, Father John turns his wrath on Father Hugh in a violent criticism of *his* lack of love and pastoral concern:

Do you even know their names? Or do you let that Polish comedian you've got in your house with you take care of that end of it? . . . Is it even a parish to you? I doubt it. You're just there, like a chaplain in a rest home. Ready to be consulted if the occasion arises. But as far as actually bringing anything *to* them, as far as actually working to make your parish any kind of living breathing spiritual community —well, how about that, Hugh? Yet isn't that just what we were enjoined to do? Most solemnly? Years ago? All of us? And how much good do *you* do them? Sitting up in a bedroom reading Newman and being grateful to God that YOU HAVE COME THROUGH. . . . I may have turned my back on my parish, but you've never even turned your face on yours. . . . You don't do your job, either. Only you don't do yours in a slightly different way.

Father Hugh is hurt by this unexpected attack, which comes from an old friend and which is directed at his "vulnerable spot"; for the charges are true, and he is forced to hear them presented bluntly. Father Hugh had been established as being aloof from his parishioners and as being content that they "keep their distance." Father Hugh had previously realized that he was not giving attention to the parish, but had rationalized that this decrepit church was merely a recuperative way station on his "road to recovery" so that he could more fully take up his priestly duties later in a better parish. But Father John punctures this illusion by pointing out Father Hugh's romantic dream of living in the past, in the good old days before Dave Kennedy died, when Father Hugh was "successful" in a "good" Irish parish. Because of this personal quest to recapture a bygone happiness, Father Hugh had been anticipating a future reward, a better parish from the bishop, and has been neglecting the present. Such indifference and apathy toward the parishioners is linked here, by Father Carmody, with his own misanthropy.

In Martin Buber's terms, Father Hugh has lost the "I-Thou" relationship with his people and is treating them, indifferently, as objects. Or as Joseph Fletcher has stated it: "The lack of love is *indifference*, not hate, and the work of love is the active will to contribute to the neighbor's well-being."

After returning from this intense confrontation with Father

John, Father Hugh dines with Father Danowski, who, in his table conversation regarding the details of the parishioners he has visited, unwittingly underscores the same theme. Father Hugh had earlier recognized Father Danowski's zeal, but now he suddenly realizes the young curate's subtle kindness in passing on the parish news to him. Alone in his room after dinner, Father Hugh meditates on the afternoon's conversation and, with his own introspective analysis, agrees with the bitter words directed against him earlier. Using the analogy of the paternalistic antebellum plantation owner who treated his slaves with "decency and kindness" but who "didn't regard them as human being," Father Hugh comes to a new realization of self, a truthful encounter with the reality of his own position: "It was a truth I should have faced up to long ago, but I'd smothered it, hadn't admitted it, and drifted along lazily, on the whole pleasantly, with a whole part of my being numbed and no longer in use: a semi-pastor, a half-priest."

His reverie is interrupted once more by a telephone call from Helen with *"dreadful"* news. Expecting that old Charlie has died, Father Hugh is shocked to hear instead that Father John is dead from a sudden ulcer hemorrhage.

Chapter Twelve is the denouement of the novel as the Carmody clan gathers together again for John's wake. The minor characters—Dan, P.J. and Bucky, Julia, Ted and Alice, Frank—are briefly completed in the opening scene. Afterwards, Father Hugh meets with Helen in a more extended conversation which first deals with John's misunderstanding of his father's real love and pride that have been hidden under the gruff surfaces. Among John's complaints against his father was the charge that Charlie's tyranny had forced Helen into an unhappy marriage with Frank; as Helen talks of this marriage, she reveals her earlier love for Hugh. Father Hugh confesses that he, too, had loved her; but he has had no regrets about his choice of the priesthood.

Old Charlie is handled separately in a later street-corner encounter in which he tries awkwardly to deny his "deathbed confession" to Father Hugh. This evasion of truth by Charlie, who is acting now as a foil, is in sharp contrast to Father Hugh's attitude. The priest has reached a new, truthful insight into his own situation; but Charlie is last seen attempting to maintain his own self-deceit. Critics who claim O'Connor sentimentalizes this old slumlord apparently fail to recognize that Charlie's dishonest position is juxtaposed between two major scenes in which Father Hugh's integrity is emphasized by his recognition of an unpleasant truth about himself. Some readers, of course, might be disappointed that Charlie, the old hypocrite, was not "suitably punished" at the end of the novel; but it seems to be a reasonable and realistic solution to his character that he is seen again creating his own world of illusions.

This illusion-reality theme is important in the novel. It appears most obviously in Charlie Carmody's avoidance of reality and in Father Kennedy's recognition of it, but every other character can be seen in terms of his fantasies. Dan, the effervescent, unsuccessful salesman, constantly creates illusions of success; Julia is obsessed with memories of her dead husband; Bucky spends his time planning a magnificent funeral for himself; Frank, the gladhanding doctor, keeps up a phony lightheartedness to defend himself from Charlie; Roy, the half-witted parish caretaker, lives in a fantastic imaginary world; Father Danowski naïvely dreams of restoring the doomed slum parish; Ted's crass political ambition blinds him to the real humanness of the older generation. To underscore this theme, there is even a long digressive story about the backsliding priest at the Cenacle, a cheerful gregarious man who will not confront the reality of his own alcoholism.

Those characters who do understand reality are given an especially sympathetic treatment. The bishop, for instance, in a few brief scenes, emerges as a just and kind administrator, competent and tolerant, who has knowledge and wisdom. Father John Carmody, for all his misanthropy, is presented as a pathetic, almost admirable, figure because he does know the truth about himself. Finally, Helen is presented as the long-suffering good woman, keeping up a cheerful civility, and yet truthfully recognizing that it is a mask and that she, too, is touched by an "edge of sadness."

Father Hugh Kennedy's own regeneration is seen in the final pages of the novel when the bishop offers him a "better" parish, a return to the Irish-Catholic world of his youth. Father Hugh wavers briefly. His desire to get back to his own past is still there; and, even after he makes his decision not to leave his slum parish, he feels a "touch of regret, an edge of sadness." But he stays with his decision with an awareness of a new joy and excitement that, "as a priest in old Saint Paul's, working day by day in this parish I had really been shamed into choosing by the scornful words of a dying friend, I might, through the parish and its people, find my way not again to the simple engagement of the heart and affections, but to the Richness, the Mercy and immeasurable Love of God. . . ."

III Critical Response and The Context of "Catholic Literature"

In general, the novel was well received by the public. During the first eight months, the hardcover edition went through five printings; in the following few years, the paperback edition had eleven printings. The book was a selection of the Book-of-the-Month Club, the Reader's Digest Condensed Books, the Catholic Book Club, the Catholic Literary Foundation, and the Thomas More Book Club. But critical reaction was extremely mixed. The initial reviews were sharply divided and, even after the book had received the Pulitzer Prize (1962), there were those who doubted the motive for this award. Some felt that the 1962 prize was sort of a "consolation prize" to O'Connor because, according to literary gossip, The Last Hurrah had been the leading contender in 1956, a year in which no award was made because of a judges' deadlock.

Although the novel was recognized by some reviewers as a major achievement in the realistic portrayal of a priest, other reviewers found it merely an entertaining "re-hash" of the Irish-Catholic world of The Last Hurrah: Frank Skeffington had metamorphosed into Charlie Carmody and that was that. Such an error is understandable. The book, after all, begins with Father Hugh's disclaimer: "This story at no point becomes my own. I am in it— good heavens, I'm in it to the point of almost never being out of it— but the story belongs, all of it, to the Carmodys, and my own part, while substantial enough, was never really of any great significance at all. I don't think this is modesty; it seems to me a simple fact."

Such a frank admission of status, together with the many episodes centering on Charlie and the Carmody family, plus O'Connor's previous reputation in creating Frank Skeffington who dominates The Last Hurrah, caused many reviewers to take the bait and to assume that Charlie Carmody is the main character.

Read in this manner, the unwary reader might even be tempted to say that "despite promising materials, nothing happens in *The Edge of Sadness*"—as did J. G. Dunne in the *National Review* of October 7, 1961 (239). But a great deal does happen; and, for the reader (who has learned not to believe everything that the first-person narrator tells about himself) who focuses on Father Hugh Kennedy as the protagonist, a subtle and highly dramatic conflict emerges as the priest reaches a crisis in his life.

It is extremely important to establish who the protagonist is in this novel. For if one does select Charlie as the main character, as some critics have, the book can be seen as "a re-write, for one thing, of O'Connor's first novel [sic]" in which "a landlord is substituted for a politician as the main character" and the novel becomes a "study of colorful Irish-American personality" with a nostalgia for a vanishing world. If "Father Kennedy has nothing to do except observe the Carmodys," then the critic might reasonably classify it as escapist literature, interesting and amusing, but not concerned with the "joy and terror of human existence"—in fact, even as presenting a "cynical and sentimental" moral vision because of its sympathy for a rogue. From such a vantage point, one could conclude that the success of the book stems from its ability to "insulate from reality" (J. McCudden, *Perspectives*, January, 1962, 26–27).

Again, if Charlie Carmody is seen as the main character, the book can be dismissed as "not much of a novel . . . in fact, probably isn't one at all . . . more like a long-winded tribute to the past, a nostalgic closeup of some Boston Irish types" (Oona Sullivan, *Jubilee*, September, 1961 (42). Certainly, a troubling concern for those who have focused so intensely on Charlie Carmody as the protagonist is the fact that the "climactic" scene, in which the supposedly dying Charlie reveals his motive for cultivating Father Kennedy's friendship, occurs one hundred pages from the end of the novel, and Charlie is rarely seen afterwards. If Charlie is the protagonist, this lengthy anticlimax is difficult to explain except in terms of poor craftsmanship, as the myopic review in *Time* (June 9, 1961,) suggested: "All Charlie wants from Father Kennedy is a crumb of assurance to feed his lonely vanity. He gets it; but it is scarcely a plausible motivation for the book-length relationship between the two men" (90).

But the book is Father Hugh's story, whether he, as narrator, denies it or not. It is the story of the regeneration of a priest, a story of sanctity in the modern world, of a man coming to terms with himself and with God. Granville Hicks, in *Saturday Review* (June 10, 1961), recognized the importance of the introductory narrative device; speaking of Father Hugh's disclaimer, Hicks noted: "This is not quite accurate, for what happens to Father Kennedy turns out to be of first importance. . . . O'Connor blends his themes skillfully, for it is by way of the Carmodys that Father Kennedy is restored to participation in life. Although it is John, the rebellious priest, who speaks the decisive words, they all help, and not least old Charlie. . . . *The Edge of Sadness* has less excitement in it than *The Last Hurrah* and it may not be so popular, but I think it is a sounder piece of work" (20).

Thus the crux of any evaluation of the *intrinsic* merit of this novel lies in the *recognition* of the protagonist and the main conflict of the story. However, in addition to an intrinsic evaluation of this work, one can also judge *The Edge of Sadness* in a wider context—in terms of its place in religious literature, or an even wider cultural context. Here the critic's familiarity with the context and traditions of religious literature can give valuable insights into the achievement of this novel.

Several critics, knowledgeable of Catholic literary traditions, pointed out the importance of O'Connor's realistic treatment of the clergy. Thomas McDonnell, in *The Critic* (July, 1961), called Father Kennedy "the first dimensionally human priest to emerge from the pages of an American novel" (18). The review in *Information* (July, 1961,) claimed that what emerged from this novel "may be that elusive and long-sought, rounded portrait of an American priest" (52). And Stephen Ryan, in *The Catholic World* (October, 1961,) surveyed the recent literary appearances of priests and noted O'Connor's contribution (49). These evaluations of *The Edge of Sadness* as being the first realistic priest-novel in American writing are correct, but they hardly suggest the significance of this fact to American literature. Ryan's list of writers, for example, puts several European writers together with James T. Farrell (who was writing from a vantage point "outside" the Church) and with J. F. Powers (who was writing from "within" the Church), and smilingly dismisses the stereotype of the "frustrated third baseman." Yet, putting things in proportion and in historical perspective, it is this *popular stereotype* which *dominated* American Catholic ghetto literature for nearly a century.

Within the American Catholic commuity, the priest-novel was the central genre of its literature and a fixed stereotype developed. This stereotype is most conveniently seen in Henry Morton Robinson's *The Cardinal*, or in movies such as *Going My Way*: but this stereotype appeared in scores of minor novels and hundreds of short stories written from within the American Catholic community.

The American Catholic ghetto stereotype of the priest (differing far from any European Catholic image) pictured the priest as an authoritarian leader, a busy executive, a competent administrator, a wise counselor and shepherd to his flock, a gregarious extrovert, an "athlete," and a heroic celibate.

This pattern, plus several negative qualities (*not* an intriguer, a lecher, or a parasite), appeared consistently throughout American Catholic ghetto writing, and also, according to the sociological studies done by Father Joseph Ficter (*Religion as an Occupation, Priest and People*) was the dominant image held by the Catholic laity and priests alike in this era. Here the literature closely reflected the commonly held assumptions of the ghetto culture. For many reasons, the early generations of Catholic immigrants had an extremely defensive mentality, hostile to their American environment, and were linked very closely to their parish churches. The priest, as local leader of the people, was exalted in status; his image took on a "halo effect" (a sociological term, most appropriate for this stereotype), an inflated ideal type.

As long as this stereotype existed within the American Catholic community, the effect of it on the writings produced there was deadening, producing sentimental stories, parochial special-pleading, and *romances* in which the idealized priest-hero was in conflict with *external* antagonists. Because of the extreme defensive mentality within American Catholicism, the recognition of one's own fallibility, as might be found in realistic literature or in satire, did not appear in the literature produced by American writers who remained within Catholicism. For example, a *novel*, as we know it with its emphasis on *inner* conflict, about a priest-protagonist simply could not exist in this atmosphere in which this highly-inflated image of the priest denied any inner conflict.

Although several major American writers (Ernest Hemingway,

F. Scott Fitzgerald, Theodore Dreiser, James T. Farrell, Eugene O'Neill) had been baptized Catholics, and had shown some indication of religious concerns in their writing, it is significant that all of them had dropped out, in one way or another, from the Catholic Church. To many, it seemed that the Catholicism that they knew was simply not compatible with their attempt to write honestly.

But American Catholicism was changing. The ghetto mentality was receding as subsequent generations Americanized, as the educational and occupational levels increased, and as the actual geographic ghettoes of the immigrants disintegrated. These factors are commonly discussed in the history of American immigration; but what is not frequently realized is the more-recent ideological shift within Catholicism itself, the emergence of a liberal Catholicism, which will have far-reaching effects on the culture and the literature of American Catholics. The emergence of a liberal spirit in Europe was at least a generation or two ahead of its appearance in America; and an important factor to consider is that much of the liberal influence was transmitted to this country through literature and related literary media (*Commonweal* magazine) rather than through any official ("conservative") ecclesiastical structures.

Edwin O'Connor was very knowledgeable about these traditions and changes within the Church and "Catholic literature." In fact, O'Connor's close friend and mentor at Notre Dame, Professor Frank O'Malley, the man to whom *The Edge of Sadness* was dedicated, was one of the men most responsible for the introduction of the *avant-garde* European Catholic writers into the American Catholic community. For years, at Notre Dame, the charismatic Professor O'Malley taught a "Modern Catholic Writers" course; and he had also helped to organize the Catholic Renascence Society, a national association of Catholic academics and others who shared the belief that a genuine "Catholic literature," in contrast to the parochial ghetto writing, was on the verge of a re-birth in the twentieth century. While few of these scholars ever agreed on the definition of "Catholic literature," the question was frequently debated in the literate Catholic magazines (*Commonweal, America*; later, *The Critic, Renascence*, etc.). These debates usually concluded, vaguely, that there was such a thing and that "Catholic literature" was involved with the basic world view of the writer, not merely with subject matter, with sectarian practices, or with prejudices.

Frank O'Malley's course, which O'Connor took as a student and in which he appeared several times later as a guest lecturer, introduced Notre Dame students to the surge of creative spirit of those French and British writers whose religious beliefs were infused deeply into their works: the novelists, François Mauriac (*The Desert of Love, The Woman of the Pharisees*); Leon Bloy (*The Woman Who Was Poor*); Georges Bernanos (*The Diary of a Country Priest*); the dramatist, Paul Claudel (*The Tidings Brought to Mary*); the painter, Georges Rouault; the philosophers, Jacques and Raissa Maritain; the men of letters, G. K. Chesterton and Hilaire Belloc, the "Chesterbelloc" foes of G. B. Shaw; the radical artisan, Eric Gill; and later, the novelists, Evelyn Waugh (*Brideshead Revisted,*) and Graham Greene (*The Power and the Glory.*) These were the "Modern Catholic Writers" of O'Mally's course; although some, by our contemporary standards, would not now be considered very "liberal," in the context of American Catholicism of the 1930's and 1940's, their writings seemed radical. The American discovery of those European writers who were combining both literary craftsmanship and their religious faith excited many of those who wished to reconcile the differences; to write well and yet to remain within the Church might be possible after all.

The first fruits in American literature of this upheaval within American Catholicism appeared in 1947 when two young writers, both of whom were seriously influenced by the radical *Catholic Worker* movement, published books which violently departed from the traditional Catholic ghetto literature: Harry Sylvester's *Moon Gaffney,* and J. F. Powers' *Prince of Darkness.* Sylvester, a recent Notre Dame graduate, produced an excoriating attack (unequalled in its vehemence until the birth-control controversy in 1965 which managed to set a few rhetorical records) on the hypocrisy and bigotry within the Catholic community; unfortunately, his literary control did not equal his reforming zeal. In contrast, J. F. Powers' short stories were models of literary craftsmanship as carefully controlled satires of priests and other Catholics. Powers' influence in this area of religious literature is undeniably important; however, he himself has limited his production to a relatively small body of stories (*The Presence of*

Grace, 1956; *Morte D'Urban,* 1962, the National Book Award novel) and to a severly restricted world.

In this context of American Catholic literature, Edwin O'Connor would be the next major writer, the first major novelist, to reflect the influence of the emergence of liberal Catholicism and the disintegration of the old ghetto mentality. In addition to the commonly perceived strengths in O'Connor's writing—the dialogue, the characterization, the strong narrative line—one must consider also that O'Connor deals with significant ideas. Among other things in this novel, he is concerned with the present status of the Catholic Church in America. Like J. F. Powers, he is a critic of the follies and foibles of the traditional Establishment, its pietistic devotionalism, its triumphalistic parochialism, and its phony images of religion and the religious. Satire, expressed through the narrator's analysis or through the dialogue, appears frequently; but, although O'Connor and Powers often share the same targets for their barbs, O'Connor lacks the sustained irony for which Powers is noted. O'Connor often seems the more "solemn" of the two, but to discuss or to evaluate these two different approaches and attitudes of critical satire, without emphasizing O'Connor's strength in creating realistic fiction, would be to slight his achievement. Powers is the better satirist, but O'Connor is less interested in satire *per se;* the satire in *The Edge of Sadness* seems to accompany rather than to dominate the story; and it serves a valid function in helping to establish the characterization of the protagonist, Father Kennedy.

A more detailed analysis of O'Connor's satire and his departure from the traditional ghetto stereotype of the priest can be found in my article "O'Connor's Image of the Priest" in the *New England Quarterly,* of March, 1968. But here it is sufficient to indicate that O'Connor's criticism of the clergy is not a sign of disaffection or anti-clericalism; it is essentially a reflection of the more liberal attitudes within the Church.

In contrast to H. M. Robinson's *The Cardinal,* which is the epitome of the American ecclesiastical "success story" (the poor boy who, through pluck and luck, works his way up the churchly ladder to worldly success), O'Connor's story is one of spiritual success that is accomplished by a renunciation of a "bigger and better" parish. Father Kennedy here joins the company of other American literary characters (Martin Arrowsmith, Biff Loman, and others) who renounce the false dream and forsake a society interested in "success." The reader has the realization that Father Kennedy will not return to his former role as organizer of the parish's bazaars and bingo games; he will concentrate on spiritual leadership and service to his people.

Out of context, the final scene could have been trite or could have been reduced to the level of a sentimental cliché about the priest-martyr who gives up the world for God. This renunciation occurs in dozens of saccharine stories in religious periodicals where, after six pages of frenzied activity, the priest-hero renounces the world; in film versions, an invisible angel chorus usually sings in the background. But some men *do* give up the world for God; the problem of the novelist is to make such a story convincing, especially to those skeptics who have seen so many two-dimensional characters, pious frauds, which have been offered to readers as "saints." Father Hugh Kennedy's choice, however, has been prepared for by over four hundred pages of honest writing and subtle characterization. After a dark night of the soul, not of alcoholism but of apathy, his choice becomes not a negative masochism but a positive commitment to duty, to love, and to God.

Such idealism is rare in the contemporary novel; the book is apt to be dismissed by many who object not so much to O'Connor's craft as to this positive value judgment. O'Connor has written a realistic Christian novel of hope in a non-Christian age when most "realists" are pessimists or nihilists. If idealism is rare in contemporary literature, realism is even rarer in the religious novel, which has had a long-standing reputation for a bland optimism. The expression of faith, in a faithless age, is a difficult task because too many Pollyannas have debased the meaning of hope. Edwin O'Connor, in this novel, joins the company of Graham Greene, François Mauriac, and Georges Bernanos as a competent creative artist who writes from a Christian ideological position. In American literature, O'Connor joins J. F. Powers as a leader in breaking away from a priestly stereotype which had dominated for nearly a century.

Schlesinger's later evaluation in *The Best and The Last of Edwin O'Connor* recognized the central importance of this novel to O'Connor's works: "O'Connor fused his two themes—the search for grace and the end of Irish America—into a single text. It is technically an impressive work, more complex in its construction and precise in its writing than *The Last Hurrah*." After summarizing the novel, Schlesinger (p. 20) noted its differences from "the conventional Catholic novel" and said that O'Connor's observations of the Church and the clergy were "notably detached and unsentimental." For all of its melancholy, Schlesinger (p. 21) said, "*The Edge of Sadness* is perhaps the most affirmative of O'Connor's novels. . . . It remained his own favorite among his novels."

CHAPTER 8

I Was Dancing

I Background

A FEW months after *The Edge of Sadness* won the Pulitzer Prize, Edwin O'Conor married Veniette Caswell Weil on September 2, 1962. Although his friends, as Schlesinger noted, had thought him to be "an incorrigible Irish bachelor," O'Connor had met Veniette the previous year at Wellfleet and the two were well suited for each other. One major problem loomed at first: O'Connor was a devout, practicing Catholic; Veniette was a divorcee with a ten-year-old son, Stephen. Initially it seemed that there might be a religious obstacle to their marriage. Later, after O'Connor's death, both his wife and his mother felt that, if an ultimate decision had had to be made by him at that time, if he had had to choose between marriage and his faith, he would probably not have married. But this anticipated crisis never materialized; ecclesiastical law did not recognize Veniette's previous civil marriage, and there were no obstacles from the Church. The O'Connors were married by Ed's old friend, Monsignor Francis J. Lally, editor of Boston's diocesan newspaper.

According to the testimony of his friends, O'Connor's marriage fulfilled him. Schlesinger (p. 27) wrote that "one feels that marriage had accelerated his process of self-exploration and self-knowledge" and Monsignor Lally, years later when reviewing *The Best and the Last of Edwin O'Connor* for the *Boston Globe* of February 22, 1970, emphasized this development: "O'Connor was always, as I remember him, a happy man, though not without his moments of Irish melancholy. After his marriage, however, happiness shone out of him as if he had swallowed the sun. The end came suddenly, but at a time when he had lived life richly and fully, with a happy home and hosts of friends" (78).

The impact of O'Connor's marriage on his writings may be seen in all of his later writings, especially in relationship to the development of female characters. It is most obvious in *All in the Family* and in the unpublished play, *The Traveler from Brazil*. But even in *I Was Dancing*, which is practically devoid of onstage female characters, one can recognize that Tom's situation has been complicated by his (absent) wife's ultimatum. While O'Connor has not attempted to characterize the wife more fully, he is aware of some counter claims for affection which do exist in married life. Perhaps part of the explanation of this "half way compromise" lies in the probability that this story had germinated in his mind years earlier. Seven years earlier, O'Connor had published a short story, "A Grand Day for Mr. Garvey," in the *Atlantic* of October, 1957, a story which centered on a wit duel between an old codger sent to a rest home and his "unfeeling" young niece. The similarity of the basic situation suggests that this theme had been long in O'Connor's mind.

I Was Dancing was first written as a play. It is important to recall O'Connor's lifelong fascination with the theater: a favorite uncle had been a vaudeville actor, as had been O'Connor's friend from Coast Guard days, Louis Brems. O'Connor himself had been in the drama club in high school; throughout his life he had a flair for mimicry which he constantly practiced. For years, he had been a radio-television critic, as "Roger Swift" and in the *Atlantic* articles; he had written radio scripts himself during his radio career and during his time as a Coast Guard information specialist; he was thoroughly familiar with Fred Allen's scripts which he had edited for *Treadmill to Oblivion*; the first sketches for *The Oracle* had been outlined as a play; some of his close friends from Wellfleet were prominent in the theater—Abe Burrows (*How to Succeed in Business Without Really Trying*) and William Gibson (*Two for the Seesaw*); and O'Connor's favorite pastime was going to the movies and the theater in Boston. In a sense, he was "stage struck." Now he seemingly wanted to achieve the same kind of recognition and success as a dramatist that he had as a novelist.

Although the playscript for *I Was Dancing* was written first, O'Connor revised it into the novel which was published in March, 1964, before the play actually appeared on Broadway in November. The Broadway production, by David Merrick, which ran for seventeen performances, starred Burgess Meredith (Daniel), who was supported by Orson Bean (Tom), David Doyle (Billy Ryan), Eli Mintz (Gottlieb), Bernard Hughes (Fr. Feeley), and Pert Kelton (Delia). The play was not well received. *Time* (November 20, 1964), for example, complained of its superfluous talk (81), and *Newsweek* (November 23, 1964) spent even more space in dissecting the play's weaknesses, describing the characters as being desperately in search of a plot and ending up as "vaudevillians, each doing his bit and then giving way to the next act" (102). In retrospect, Eliot Norton would recall that Burgess Meredith played Daniel "erratically"; Schlesinger (p. 23) was more emphatic about Meredith's acting: "his free, sometimes forgetful, way with the lines drove Ed to distraction." O'Connor's first full-scale foray into theater was a failure; afterwards, he said to Eliot Norton, "I'm a novelist. I'm not a playwright" (reported in Norton's *Record American* column, March 6, 1970). But, he would try again three years later with *The Traveler From Brazil.*

II *The Novel*

Divided into seven chapters, the novel *I Was Dancing* shows its origin as a play as it adheres closely to the unities of time, place, and action. The whole story takes place in one day in early September, 1962; the first three chapters occur in the morning, the next three in the afternoon, all leading up to the final confrontation in the evening. Nearly two-thirds of the "scenes" within the novel are located in Daniel's room. A rather detailed summary seems necessary, primarily to demonstrate the coherence and the functional contributions of certain characters and scenes which have been criticized by some as being unconnected.

The opening chapter alternates its focus between the two main characters and reveals the conflict between them. Daniel Considine, a seventy-eight-year-old ex-vaudevillian, had returned after a twenty-year absence to visit his grown son, Tom; the old man had extended his "visit" for nearly a year and now plans to make this his "home." Tom, pressured by his wife's insistence, is trying to evict his father, to move him to Saint Vincent's Smiling Valley for Senior Citizens. The story takes place on the day which had been set as a deadline for the eviction; Tom's wife is away, visiting relatives in another city. As the story opens, Daniel is going through his complicated morning ritual of moving about his room, puttering around, and making sounds which disturb Tom, not because of the actual noise involved, but because of the unexplained nature of Daniel's daily ritual. For the past year, these mysterious little sounds have been a source of annoyance and exasperation to Tom because Daniel is apparently trying to attract attention and, at the same time, frustrating any attempt to solve the mystery.

Daniel's ritual is revealed to the reader as the old man is shown getting out of bed, measuring himself at the mirror to check that he hasn't shriveled up, and then going through an elaborate game of pretending that he is back on the vaudeville circuit again. Rushing around the room at full speed, he packs his imaginary suitcases and props just as he had done every morning in various hotels during the fifty years of one-night stands in vaudeville. With a huge theatrical poster on the wall announcing "WALTZING DANIEL CONSIDINE!" as a backdrop for his imaginary flights, Daniel recaptures his glorious past as a vaudeville star. After such sentimental reminiscences, the practical side of his egocentricity is revealed. When his ritual is completed, he returns to bed until noon to rest, to take care of himself, and to re-read his scrapbooks.

While these actions are being described, O'Connor is doing a great deal of characterization of Daniel through frequent asides about his attitudes toward his son and daughter-in-law. The fractiousness of this crotchety old man is developed humorously through these insights into his self-rightous viewpoint. When the telephone rings during his morning ritual, Daniel answers it and abruptly hangs up: "Some time ago he had decided to answer all calls for his son and his daughter-in-law by denying that they were in or available. He did this out of fairness to himself. *Because what the hell am I*, he thought indignantly, *a damn messenger boy? At my age?*"

Tom sees his father in a different light. While these opening passages do emphasize Tom's annoyance and exasperation with petty irritations, thus revealing the lack of charitable tolerance in the son, the passages also suggest two possible "faults" in the father. Tom suspects that his father might be senile, an inference drawn not only from Daniel's actions but also from some seemingly nonsensical telephone conversations which Tom has overheard. But Tom's wife, Ellen, has convinced Tom that the old man is really a very clever, cunning, calculating person and that his strange actions are not signs of senility but evidences of strategy.

The second chapter introduces Billy Ryan, the first of Daniel's cronies, who serve as the confidants to whom Daniel reveals his plans for outwitting Tom. Billy Ryan is an old eccentric who sees himself as a "Free Lancer of Medicine." He enters, carrying a physician's satchel, and makes constant references to the patients he has known and the latest scientific discoveries in medicine. He is *not* under the delusion that he is an "Official Doctor," but he believes that the medical profession labors under the delusion that only those who "have gone through medical schools and have diplomas and all that nonsense" are able to help the sick. Because Daniel, too, mistrusts doctors, these two men share a common grudge and frequently serve as good listeners for each other. Billy Ryan's enthusiastic interest in popular science parallels that of Charlie Hennessey in *The Last Hurrah,* and O'Connor goes as far as to repeat the same anecdote, used in the earlier novel, when Billy Ryan explains his idea of taking snapshot photos of hospital patients to record their physical condition.

With Billy as a sympathetic audience, Daniel retells his version of how a "vision" came to him that directed him to go and live the rest of his life at Tom's house. Daniel believes that the current problem has really been created by Tom's wife because "Tom by himself would of done nothing. He hasn't the spunk." Even though Daniel's sister, Delia, lives at the Smiling Valley home, Daniel doesn't want to go to an "Old Man's Home": "I know those Smiling Valleys. A bowl of thin soup in the mouth and a thermometer up the behind twice a day. And everybody out there shuffling around, all held together with Scotch tape and piano wire." As Billy Ryan leaves, Daniel invites him to return in the afternoon to witness "a preview of the battle plan . . . a private dress rehearsal of Waltzing Daniel Considine in action."

In the meantime, earlier in the chapter, Tom's thoughts are presented as he begins the day's work. On the way to his office, Tom meets a cranky old priest, Father McGovern, the eighty-three-year-old retired pastor of the parish. In a loud booming voice, which embarrasses Tom because bystanders overhear the conversation, the priest asks Tom some catechism questions and then inquires about Tom's marriage and family: "NO CHIL-

DREN! AFTER SEVEN YEARS OF MARRIAGE!. . . . Where's
your training? Eh? *We can't live like pagans, Bob!*" After this
meeting, Tom begins to think about the similarities between his
own father and Father McGovern: "An encounter with either was
not an easy matter; neither could be defended against by any of
the standard rational procedures. It was in part of course a question of age. Not until recently had Tom thought much about old
age; now—or so it seemed to him—he thought about it all the
time. He was suddenly surrounded by it; it seemed to him he
met a new old man every day; he had begun to realize that old
age was a strange and usually hostile world, whose ways and
weapons he did not understand at all."

Although Tom seems to think of the conflict in war-like terms
("hostile world," "weapons"), Daniel's attitude—and the omniscient
narrator's—suggests that the conflict is in terms of games and
ritualistic plays. Years before Eric Berne (in *Games People Play*)
popularized game theory, O'Connor had conceived of these psy-
chodramas as the games old people played with the young. In
"A Grand Day for Mr. Garvey," the weekly visit from the niece
was Mr. Garvey's chance to play "The Game" with her. So also,
in *I Was Dancing*, the conflict is conceived as a form of play or
ritual: "Upstairs, Daniel had already begun his little game. It
was a game he played every morning . . ."

The third chapter is composed of three telephone conversations; each of these dialogues features the auxiliary characters
who are allied with Tom in trying to get Daniel to go to Smiling
Valley. The first of the phone calls is to Tom, working at his law
office, from Brother Martin, one of the staff at Smiling Valley.
Brother Martin's conversation reveals him as a stupid, shallow
fool. Gregarious and overfamiliar, he speaks almost totally in
clichés ("cash in her chips . . . that's the way the ball bounces. . . .
I know all the ropes") and prides himself on his grossest truisms.
Some of the details suggest that O'Connor is also playing a private
joke because Brother Martin comes from Providence, Rhode Island, and had ambitions to become a writer before he settled on
his religious vocation: it is almost as if O'Connor were parodying
the man *he* himself could have been if he had followed his early
inclinations toward a religious vocation. Brother Martin had
called Tom to check on the final arrangements for Daniel's admission; but, as Tom listens to Brother Martin, who refers to

Daniel as "Dad" and expects that "Dad" is cheerfully anticipating Smiling Valley, Tom's own feelings about his father become more complex as he perceives the kind of obnoxious treatment his father will receive.

In the mid-section of the chapter, Daniel receives a call from his sister Delia who lives at Smiling Valley. As Delia nags and scolds Daniel about his irresponsibility, her self-righteous indignation serves not only to characterize her but also to reveal more about Daniel's past history. Daniel's vaudeville act was a *comic* routine in which he waltzed around the stage with an old floor mop dressed up to look like a woman; Delia "was always ashamed" to see her brother doing such an undignified thing with everyone yelling and laughing at him. Daniel counterattacks by mocking Delia's religious enthusiasm, and this mockery leads to Delia's sarcastic attack on Daniel's friend, a cynical priest, Father Feeley, whose main interest is in playing the horses. As the argument continues, Delia gloats about Daniel's eviction and ironically describes how eagerly he is anticipated at Smiling Valley. Furious, Daniel hangs up.

While the function of the first two phone calls shows the negative aspects of Daniel's move to Smiling Valley, the final phone call indicates the opposing pressure. Tom's wife, Ellen, calls Tom at the office; after some preliminary talk of her situation as an invited visitor at her sister's house in Detroit, the conversation shifts to Tom's apprehension about Brother Martin. The earlier phone call had started Tom worrying that his father would be harassed by Brother Martin, and Tom apparently is wavering in his plan to evict his father. The conversation with Ellen, however, strengthens Tom's resolve because his wife emphasizes her inability to tolerate Daniel any longer. When Daniel had first arrived, Ellen had been charmed and fascinated by him, but Daniel's "picturesqueness withered before familiarity." Her sympathy and tolerance toward Daniel faded as he remained longer and proved to be "a self-centered and determined old man who had decided to make what was hers his own." Although no actual arguments ever occurred, Daniel's omnipresence in the house, as if he had taken over, disturbed Ellen. Before Ellen complained, Tom had no great objection to Daniel's presence; Tom himself, easygoing, almost inert, prefered "solutions that came without his direct intervention." But now, pressured by his wife, Tom promises to go through with the eviction; the conversation (and this first act) ends with Ellen's warning that Daniel is tricky and cunning.

The fourth chapter is also divided into three major scenes which function obliquely to develop the conflict between father and son. Although Daniel and Tom are physically separated in this early afternoon period, both are mentally involved with each other in preparation for the evening's showdown. Daniel receives two visitors in his room; and both—Delia, as a hostile questioner, and Father Feeley, as a friendly witness—allow Daniel an impromptu recitation of some of his arguments. Tom, at the office, encounters another strained father-son relationship in the Pomeroy family.

In the first scene, which foreshadows the final confrontation, Delia, who acts as the accuser, berates Daniel for his long absence, his desertion of the family, and his gall for expecting to be sheltered now by Tom and Ellen. Although the argument seems to ramble, it is actually a series of diversions, by *ad hominum* counterattacks, by Daniel parrying the accusations made by Delia. For example, when Delia denounces Daniel's worthless friends, Daniel implies that she's jealous because she is unpopular, an ugly duckling. But his sarcasm doesn't work, and Delia's attack continues as she reminds him of reality: "You're not in Loew's State Theater now. You're in real life and you've got to face facts." When Delia returns to her denunciations of Daniel's past errors, she adds insult to her account of his life by misnaming some of Daniel's treasured memories. She says *Dancing* Daniel Considine instead of *Waltzing*, and she speaks of his trip to *Venezuela* instead of *Australia*. Daniel's ego and his sense of order are more disturbed by these errors than by her arguments about his paternal behavior.

When Delia points out Ellen's objection to Daniel, he replies "Who gives a damn what she will or she won't do. She hasn't the say; it's not her house. It's Tom's house, and if you have to be reminded again, Tom's my son." The implied premises of this statement reveal Daniel's patriarchal concept of family structure, for such male authoritarianism sees the father as sole owner, director, and boss of his wife and children. Although Daniel recognizes that Tom is titular head of his own house now, Daniel expects sufference from him almost in the sense of "professional courtesy" among fellow despots.

Then, Delia, in effect, challenges Daniel's basic claim to father-hood: "He's been your son for more than forty years, and the only times he saw you was between trains!" Unable to refute this criticism, Daniel makes his first concession, "All right: I wasn't home much. I could of stayed home more." But he immediately justifies his prolonged absences as beneficial both to himself and to the family because his constant traveling kept him from a futile life—"going nowhere and seeing nothing"—and from fighting with his wife, Rose. He concludes his defense by emphasizing that he had always provided for his family and that Tom owes him a debt of gratitude for this: "And as far as Tom goes, I might not of seen him much, but I supported him damn well. He went to the best schools money could buy, and he went to them all the way. All right, so I wasn't at hand every blessed minute, but what I made was. And don't ever forget this: what he's got today he owes to one man, Me!"

Delia shifts ground to point out the more general idea of the gap between the young and the old: "We're too slow for them, we mix up their lives, we get in the way." But Daniel is unmoved by her final persuasions, and he invites her to return in the evening to witness the confrontation. Father Feeley's knock at the door interrupts their conversation; a brief transition exchange between Delia and the priest shows their mutual scorn for each other.

After Delia leaves, Father Feeley and Daniel discuss the attrac-tion of Delia and her kind of "harpies" to religion: "Sooner or later," Father Feeley says, "they all turn to religion. . . . They settle down on priests like vampire bats." But, he continues, "I hold the diocesan record for getting rid of women like your sis-ter." Changing the subject to Daniel's problem, Father Feeley asks the simple basic question, *why* does Daniel want to stay at Tom's. Daniel replies: "Because it's my home, that's why. Every man's got to have a home at last!" Further development of this idea is diverted by Daniel who suspects that Delia is eavesdrop-ping at the door. While Daniel's secret codes for door knocking and his frequent checking of the door for unseen listeners may be suggestive of a mild persecution complex, these things also serve Daniel well as very natural devices by which he can usually divert attention from the issue at hand.

While Daniel checks the door, Father Feeley's ironic comments about Daniel's actions indicate that the priest has a strange relationship with Daniel, a mixture of a cynical appreciation and of condescending fascination. Throughout the scenes in which the priest appears, he uses an ironic sarcasm which frequently is directed at Daniel. Daniel, however, does not comprehend, or will not acknowledge to himself, that many of the priest's subtle barbs are aimed his way. Generally, Daniel finds the priest a congenial friend and admires his brusque manner.

Meanwhile, Tom, at a bar near his office, meets an old college friend, Jack Pomeroy, the son of Tom's boss. The old Mr. Pomeroy, the senior partner at the law firm, never speaks of his son; Jack Pomeroy, however, "had long spells in which he spoke of little else but his father." Jack, who is extremely bitter about his father, sees him as a greedy man and as a phony who pretends to be an "old fashioned" lawyer when in reality he is "as homespun as General Dynamics." Tom doesn't understand why the older Pomeroy is taking on an unprofitable divorce case; Jack explains the old man's probable motives in terms of a long-harbored grudge. Through this insignificant legal case, Mr. Pomeroy will be able to revenge himself on the Beckwith family which had caused his political defeat thirty years ago. Although the complicated history of the Beckwith divorce case does not relate directly to the main plot, the conversation serves to underline the parallel father-son conflict and to remind Tom that his own father's money was the reason "he had met Jack, and Jack's world, later at a succession of conservative and expensive boarding schools." Afterwards, thinking about this talk, Tom realizes "with something of a shock that this was the only meeting or conversation he had had all day in which his father had not been mentioned. Yet, curiously, nothing in the day had made him think of his father more. . . ." The chapter ends with this emphasis on Tom's growing sense of obligation to his father for sending him to the best schools.

The fifth chapter is set in Daniel's room in the late afternoon. Father Feeley is still there talking with Daniel; another friend, Gottlieb, soon arrives; and Billy Ryan later returns—thus providing Daniel with a full-house audience of old cronies as he presents a dress rehearsal of what he plans to do that evening with Tom. As the chapter opens, Daniel and Father Feeley are talking about Gottlieb's background. Gottlieb, the faithful husband and father, had been betrayed both by his wife, who ran off with an exotic musician, and by his son, who had become a Hollywood celebrity. The crushing blow to Gottlieb occurred while he was living with his son and daughter-in-law in Hollywood; at a party, the son humiliates the father by mocking him. Insulted by this rejection, Gottlieb leaves their household and now spends his time lamenting about his fate and the injustice done to him.

Gottlieb arrives. An atypical character in O'Connor's writings, Gottlieb seems to be straight out of Yiddish humor where such a *shlimazl*, a chronically unlucky person, is commonplace. Gottlieb immediately starts relating his latest misfortunes—the car broke down on the way over, a good friend dropped dead yesterday—and, while he insists that he can't say a word about his wife and son, he retells his version of his favorite story of himself as the long-suffering martyr in the family. Gottlieb's complaint is counterpointed by Father Feeley's sardonic comments. Gottlieb offers his experience as a warning to Daniel that sons can often turn on their good fathers, but Daniel rejects the implications: "Not if you know how to handle them right."

When Billy Ryan returns, his pseudo-medical chatter is directly mocked by Father Feeley, who has more experience and less tolerance with him than the others. But, before an argument can develop, Daniel begins to dominate the conversation, reminding his friends that they had come to witness a rehearsal of his meeting with Tom. Daniel begins to tell his plan, saying that he is going to use the strategy of silence: he will open the door for Tom, be silent, and look sad. Tom, in grief and guilt, will capitulate. When the three cronies are disappointed and when each argues that the plan is not good enough, Daniel quickly agrees and tells them that he has been withholding the best part, whereupon Daniel goes into a pantomime of an old man trembling, having a bad case of the shakes. A pathetic sight, they all agree, and they begin to congratulate him on his acting ability. Suddenly, Daniel begins to gasp: "Without warning, his speech broke off into a choking, gurgling sound; as he uttered it Daniel bent double, then snapped back into an unnaturally stiff, erect position. His face moved as if he had no control over its expression; his tongue popped out and, gasping, he staggered, then collapsed into a chair. He lay there, sprawled out awkwardly, his breathing

deep and rasping, one leg jerking spasmodically, his arms flopping
bonelessly about."

Horrified that Daniel's pretending had tragically turned into
reality, his friends go to his aid. But, in an instant, Daniel is back
to normal again and delighted that his acting ability is so good.
The friends agree that Daniel's act is impressive, and they promise to return that evening to witness his triumph. After they leave,
Daniel, alone in the room, practices his pantomine, turns on his
record player, and dances gleefully in anticipation of the encounter.

The sixth chapter is very brief, but it serves a vital function as
it focuses on Tom's immediate preparations for the confrontation.
While Tom eats dinner at home, he hears his father shuffling
around in his room upstairs; but Tom's thoughts return to an
earlier conversation he had with Jack Pomeroy. Jack had accused
Tom of being too sentimental about Daniel. Tom, in return,
envies Jack's clear-cut attitude of "undeviating dislike" toward his
father, Mr. Pomeroy, because of the years of hostile scrutiny
from that old man. Tom's attitude is more ambiguous, a more
complicated love-hate relationship. While he didn't feel such extreme hostility toward his father, he did feel the neglect; yet, at
the same time, Daniel did have a beguiling charm about him
which Tom grudgingly liked.

Weighing the various points, Tom concludes that his decision
to send Daniel to Smiling Valley is the correct one: "there was
no question of injustice, of ingratitude: certainly all debts to his
father, even presuming they had existed, had been paid off long
ago. So then, he was behaving badly, he had no grounds for
self-reproach, for uneasiness. . . . And yet he was uneasy . . . for
the first time he would have his father at his mercy. The old positions of authority were now reversed: it was now Tom who was
calling the tune; his father could do nothing but obey." This help-
lessness of his father bothers Tom; it disturbs him that his father
should be in such a hopeless situation because, as Tom sees it,
there can be no argument at all as Tom holds all the cards. Thus,
the immediate prelude (the sixth chapter; the Second Act) to the
climax closes with the element of dynamic suspense because the
equality of the conflict has been established: both sides have exposed weaknesses, yet both sides claim superiority.

If the reader has granted the author's *donnée* and has followed the thread of father-son conflict in this story, the final confrontation, in the last chapter, is likely to be judged as one of the most intense scenes O'Connor ever created. The argument between Daniel and Tom is long and complicated, but the patterns of attack and counterattack are there underneath the surface brilliance of the dialogue; therefore, that which seems to ramble or to be redundant is, in fact, carefully structured. The first section, extending almost twenty pages, is practically a monologue; in vaudeville terms, Tom is acting as the "straight man" for Daniel's act. Within this section, there are four recognizable movements in Daniel's tactics. The opening gambit is a plea for sympathy. Daniel has painstakingly arranged the room to emphasize its barrenness; his bags are packed, and one sock is sticking out of a suitcase for "a little touch of pathos." When Tom enters, Daniel begins a slow shuffling movement and talks about his old age. Tom, deliberately silent, is wary of being caught in conversation with such a skilled talker. Daniel maneuvers his monologue, despite Tom's silence, by some clever associations: "By God, Tom . . . you'll never wear yourself out talking, will you? But that's all right, because you're a hell of a listener . . . that'd be great stuff in a courtroom . . . should of been a lawyer. . . . What the hell am I talking about? He *is* a lawyer! And who should know that better than me, the one who put him through law school?" After making his point, Daniel feigns resignation to his fate and waits for Tom's change of heart.

When Tom doesn't reply, Daniel begins his second ploy, blackmail. Talking about a television program, "Where Are They Today?" which interviews old celebrities, Daniel notes how harmful it would be to a person's career if that person's old father were to appear on the program and tell how he had been evicted from his home. Tom is relieved that Daniel had decided to be "tough rather than tearful"; and when this tactic fails, Daniel emphasizes his toughness by pointing out that *he* has always been able to take care of himself: "I didn't have anyone to take care of all my bills and bring me up and see to it that I was educated with the finest in the country." Suddenly, Daniel begins his planned pantomime—he staggers, gasps, gurgles, and goes into his "fit." Tom is unmoved. Instead of sympathy, he reproaches his father for faking: "Cut it out. It's another game. And this one

I'm not playing. . . . Fake, fake, fake. . . . It's humiliating. Degrading."

Daniel, incensed that his pantomime has failed, takes the offensive, accusing Tom of spying at his door, of beating a sick old man, and of not caring. Tom feels as if he is being drawn into the argument and then Daniel accuses him of being *cold:* "You're a cold boy and you always were." Daniel recalls that Tom, even as a baby, was cold, and that in school Tom was ungrateful. Cold, he accuses, all the way through: "cold head, cold heart, cold bones!" This accusation is the stimulus which moves Tom to an angry response, breaking his passive role as the silent observer; and the second major movement of the scene occurs as Tom launches his counterattack.

Tom responds "almost jubilantly" as if he wanted to *"pay him back"* for the years of absence and neglect. Tom concedes that Daniel provided money, but that he got out of the responsibilities of fatherhood rather cheaply: "In this city today there are twenty men, all about your age, who have no family ties with me, who have never given me a cent, who had no special reason and certainly no obligation to help me or even to like me. And yet from every one of them I've gotten more kindness, advice, assistance, and just plain human consideration than I've ever gotten from you—and to every one of them I feel closer, infinitely closer, than I do to you." Love, not money, was Tom's need; a father, not a provider, and Tom accuses Daniel of not really being a father to him: ". . . if you'd been any kind of a father at all—and I mean *any* kind. . . . I don't think I could say what I did." This outburst has been a catharsis for Tom: "He felt exhausted; he also felt ashamed. Yet at the same time he was somehow glad that he had said what he did; he would not have taken the words back. They had been necessary to him. . . ."

Daniel cools and diverts the conversation with anecdotal reminiscences of his vaudeville days, stories which eventually lead back to his role as a good provider and as a thoughtful father who always sent presents to Tom. Daniel admits that he wasn't a "palsy-walsy" kind of father and that he wasn't always around "to read bedtime stories about Bunny Rabbit Goes to the Blueberry Dump," but he does claim that he liked Tom and he reemphasizes that the presents he always sent were evidences of his concern. Tom rebuts this claim in an extended description of his memory of these presents as always being junky oddities, wrapped in old newspapers, as if they had been picked at the last minute at a souvenir counter in the railroad station. While Tom is trying to point out the lack of thoughtful selection, Daniel turns the argument and accuses Tom of being greedy: "I see where I made one hell of a mistake with you: *I forgot to give you Cadillacs!*" Weary, drained and blank, Tom feels that it is useless to try to communicate with his father now. After this argument of *unthoughtful* vs. *ungrateful*, there is a pause as Tom returns to his silence, again forcing Daniel to take a new tact.

Asking what he as a father did that was so bad, Daniel starts talking and eventually makes the concession: "ALL RIGHT! I LEFT HOME! I LEFT YOUR MOTHER! AND I LEFT YOU!" Tom stirs: "It was the first time that his father had ever admitted the fact of his desertion; it was the crack in the wall." But Daniel immediately continues, as he did earlier with Delia, with a defense—a justification of his actions. He describes himself as misunderstood at home, with a nagging wife, with an intolerable marriage situation which was eased by his absence. He admits *partial* guilt, that he "could of" come home more often; but he also argues that Tom has no right to judge him.

Tom is unmoved; he continues to stare at Daniel. The tension increases, and finally Daniel capitulates: "No maybes, I *could* of . . . I *should* of. I should of, I should of." This confession is the breaking point; Daniel has admitted full guilt. Although this is the confession for which Tom has been waiting, "this new, contrite Daniel left him strangely uneasy"; although Tom had "won," he felt himself "in a curious position of disadvantage." In effect, Tom has lost the advantage of "distance"; after Tom's initial outburst, in which he had denied that Daniel had been a father, Tom had been able to see Daniel as an old man rather than as father. Daniel's confession of fatherly guilt has created a more intimate relationship, one which carries with it the obligation for the injured party to forgive. But, in this case, forgiveness would imply non-eviction; and thus Daniel has forced Tom back into the conflict again. Now, however, Daniel has an advantage since he has admitted total guilt, but Tom's "sin" against his father has yet to be exposed. Daniel again assumes the offensive by reminding Tom of an incident from the past when Tom, in the company of his college friends, had been *ashamed* of Daniel's foolish

vaudeville routine. Tom, now on the defensive, recognizes his
guilt, confesses, and apologizes. Daniel has snapped the trap:
with the mutual apologies waiting for forgiveness, Daniel proposes that they clean the slate, start afresh, live together in the
house in a new life: "A boy and his Dad, all squared away now,
knowing each other for the first time, talking to each other like
. . . well, like real *pals!*"

As Tom comprehends what Daniel has done in this maneuver,
the final stage of argument begins. He accuses Daniel of deceit—
("The whole thing from first to last was a trick"); he rejects
Daniel's plea to be pals; he points out the inequality of their
mutual offenses; and he charges that Daniel is totally egocentric:
"you don't give a damn about me or about *my* wife." Daniel, who
is at first enraged, quickly changes to a pleading entreaty; Tom,
feeling that he is unable to communciate any more with his
father, ends the discussion by leaving the room: "I'm sorry, Dad,"
he said. "Goodbye."

After Tom leaves, Daniel is raging alone in his room when
Delia stops by to ask him if he wants a ride to Smiling Valley.
He shouts her away and then subsides into a miserable exhaustion
as he realizes that all of his resources are gone. In desperation
and panic, he begins to pray, trying to barter with God, offering
"a *ton* of Hail Marys . . ." and some money to charity if God will
only work a fast miracle to change Tom's mind. Daniel is startled
by a knock at the door, incredulous that he may have received
such an instant response from God; but, instead of a contrite son
at the door, Billy Ryan, Gottlieb, and Father Feeley have arrived
for the anticipated "victory" celebration. Daniel, taken aback,
delays opening the door, then puts on his theme song full blast
on the record player. Inviting them in, he begins dancing in
desperate gaiety: "I'm dancing for joy! Because I finally made up
my mind! Oh yes! I've got great news for you! The thing is this:
I've changed my plans!" The friends, bewildered at first, painfully comprehend the situation and Daniel's pretense. The reader,
like Tom, is apt to "grudgingly admire" Daniel, the old man's
endurance, and his desperate attempt to retain his pride and
dignity. No simple reaction is possible.

III *Critical Response*

Although most reviews agreed that *I Was Dancing* was an entertaining novel, but a lesser achievement than *The Last Hurrah* or *The Edge of Sadness*, the diversity of the critical estimate was extremely wide. At one extreme, Roger Dooley's review called this O'Connor's worst book: "In short, this thin artificially contrived, and padded effort is a veritable *reductio ad absurdum* of all the limitations implicit in the two earlier novels, here undisguised by any accidental interest of subject matter or charm of style." At the other extreme, Julian Moynahan's review praised *I Was Dancing* as "probably his best book and one of the subtlest and most suggestive novels to come out of the Hub since *The Bostonians.* . . ." Thus, the opposing views were established: while Dooley called Daniel's friends "synthetic, stylized old men . . . docile stooges," Moynahan referred to them as "a delicately stylized chorus of admirers [which] provide some of the most delightful passages of comic writing in recent memory." Although both critics started from the very same negative premise ("O'Connor cannot portray female characters"), they reached opposite conclusions as to the merit of *I Was Dancing*.

Dooley's essay, "The Womanless World of Edwin O'Connor," in the *Saturday Review* of March 21, 1964 (34–36) began by reviewing *I Was Dancing*, but it was primarily devoted to the absence of women in O'Connor's other works, especially in *The Edge of Sadness* (see Chapter 7). Although Dooley's essay does contain some valid insights, its tone is so sarcastic and intemperate that it is understandable that O'Connor was furious about this review; his friends say it provided one of the few times he so openly expressed his anger. Dooley granted the validity of the basic theme, but denied that O'Connor's characters were worth reading about: "the reader could not care less what becomes of Waltzing Daniel or of Tom, his nonentity of a son, who exists only in relation to his father, without the slightest individuality. . . . Tom has apparently been given a wife only because as a bachelor he would have no pressing reason to get rid of his father, and the author would have no pat situation." Here, Dooley correctly recognized that Tom's wife provided the "pressing reason," but he erroneously assumed that such pressure was mere contrivance; he did not comprehend the vital necessity of this pressure for Tom's inner conflict, the complications involved in this love triangle.

(In my earlier article, "O'Connor's Image of the Priest," published in the *New England Quarterly* in March, 1968, I had written: "Dooley's charges regarding the absence of female characters in *I Was Dancing* are much more convincing because the absence of Tom's wife in that story is a more crucial and less legitimate omission." On further reflection, I disagree now with my previous statement. Tom's wife need not, *should not*, be home. Her vital function is to give the ultimatum to Tom, thus catching him between two inflexible wills. If she were present, the action could logically shift to a three-cornered argument: Daniel would attempt to persuade her too, a totally different story than the crucial father-son conflict. If present and persuadable, a different story; if present and *unpersuadable*, distracting *and* superfluous.)

In contrast, to Dooley's attack, Moynahan's review, in the *New York Review of Books* of April 30, 1964 (13–14), argued that in this novel O'Connor "transcends his limitations by a process of purification and concentration . . . the plot, focusing on a fundamental conflict of interest and willing between a father and his grown-up son, is simple and archetypal." Taken as such an archetypal situation, Moynahan discussed the story in terms of wider cultural myths:

The book is very Irish (including Boston Irish) in that, at its emotional center occurs the phenomenon of the father's *unrepentant* rejection of domesticity, more particularly of the paternal role. And yet it seems very American—Anglo-Saxon American, that is—in its insistence on making the father finally accountable for behavior which no Irish Irishman would expect to have to defend. Like Joyce's Simon Dedalus, like O'Casey's Captain Boyle, and like all the devout Irish boys who each year discover they have a vocation for the celibate priesthood, Daniel has found something to do which attracts him more than looking after progeny and keeping home fires burning. But, like Hawthorne's Wakefield, like Rip Van Winkle, and even like world-waltzing Captain Ahab, Daniel simply mustn't be allowed to get away with it without paying a fine to American conscientiousness. The dullish, half-Yankified son, typifying that conscientiousness in contrast to Irish male insouciance, playing the part of "coast defender" against the father's part of pioneer-adventurer, exacts the penalty while we readers, moved and amused, ponder once again the complex fate of being what Woodrow Wilson once snobbishly called a hyphenated American.

Time and *Newsweek* also provided a matched set of opposites. *Time*, in April 10, 1964 (106), noted O'Connor's radio background and said the book sounded like a discarded sequence from "Allen's Alley" with the characters trotting on and off like a vaudeville show: "O'Connor is less interested in plot than in the smoky tank of Irish talk and in the embalmment of a cast of characters as stereotyped as Mrs. O'Leary's cow—Father McGovern, an octogenarian priest who rejoices fiercely every time a parishoner precedes him to the grave [*sic*]; Al Gottlieb, a Jewish businessman who prattles like a borscht-circuit comic." In contrast, *Newsweek* of March 23, 1964 (98), was not only more sensitive to the plot situation but also saw in Daniel an "outrageously vital hero . . . both insufferable and irresistible." The *Newsweek* reviewer suggested that the story could be viewed as a parable of the generation gap or as a study of the theatrical temperament, but it recommended that "the easy way is to take it as the story of Waltzing Daniel Considine, his family and friends—strong and subtle in its character portrayal, outlandishly funny, swift and deft in motion, another testimony to Edwin O'Connor's love and comprehension of human beings."

Two Catholic magazines also presented divergent criticisms. Father Harold C. Gardiner, writing in *America* of April 11, 1964 (516), focused on O'Connor's dialogue: "A flood of words keeps afloat, though it often threatens to overwhelm, a frail ark of story." While Gardiner was impressed by this "Niagara of talk," he felt that "the brilliance of the talk is its own end"; and he compared the book, unfavorably, to O'Connor's other works in which the talk worked closer into the action. Michael O'Malley's review in *The Critic* of April, 1964 (54–55), also praised the dialogues as "masterpieces of slightly loony magic . . . blarney played through a supremely sensitive instrument"; but O'Malley regarded the dialogue as subordinate to plot:

There is a ruthless candor to this book that was absent from the earlier novels; it is pitched higher and more sharply . . . . not here the sweet slow elegy that followed the death of Skeffington . . . nor the poignant resignation that enfolds Father Kennedy . . . now

O'Connor is dealing with father and son, with bonds that are too intimate to have much slack in them. He does it well . . . by the climax, O'Connor has created such a living, breathing *bastard* of a man that it is impossible to watch dispassionately as Tom goads his father into an abject and miserable recitation of his sins. By every rule of right and reason, old Daniel has it coming . . . [but] it is a grave disappointment to find that Tom—when he is at his best—is in essence as sterile as the old man. The judging of one's parents is a hazardous business, it would appear, and one better left alone. Tom Considine does not emerge from the attempt unscathed.

The review in the *New Yorker* of April 4, 1964, (192) was cool to the novel primarily, it seems, because of the *type* of people O'Connor chose to present: "Daniel and his ancient cronies, and Tom and his middle-aged cronies [*sic*], talk a good deal about death and fate and the gulf between the generations, but the mainspring of this novel is, in fact, merely resentment, because resentment is the strongest and most enduring emotion that these mediocre people can feel, and because it presents them at one and the same time with an excuse for their coldheartedness and a justification of their selfishness. The writing is painfully forced." Closer to home, the brief review by William Barrett, in the *Atlantic* of April, 1964 (145–46), was warm with enthusiasm for O'Connor's ability to deal with old age. Daniel was seen as a "fascinating character" and as a "crafty adversary." While noting the humor in the book, the reviewer emphasized that the "tone, beneath the occasional laughter, is almost harsh in its truthfulness. In this pathetic but impossible old man caught in the toils of his own egotism, O'Connor casts a cold and glaring light on one perennial problem of old age that neither geriatrics nor social measures can ever hope to cure."

David Dempsey's review, in the *New York Times Book Review* of March 22, 1964 (4), agreed that the novel was "a valid and uncompromising study of defeated old age." But Dempsey, a novelist himself, also illuminated some of the technical aspects in the characterization of Daniel. The *cumulative* effect of Daniel's talk serves an important function in the novel: "The author's problem is to make the old man tolerable to the reader while keeping him non grata to his son and daughter-in-law. This is not easy. Although Daniel has our sympathy in the beginning, as the day wears on he becomes more and more trying. His cunning, his wheedling importunities and self-pity, all of which display his skill as an actor, betray his limitations as a father and a man. His continual line of gab—in this case not a gift but a curse—becomes increasingly wearisome. Like Babbitt, he is too much with us, and we begin to appreciate why places like Smiling Valley have waiting lists."

Schlesinger, in *The Best and the Last of Edwin O'Connor,* borrowed from his own earlier review in the *Boston Globe* of March 24, 1964 (13), to describe the book as bearing "the same relationship to O'Connor's more serious work as, say, Graham Greene's 'entertainments' do to his novels. Like *Benjy,* it represented a lighter interlude in between major efforts." Holding to this idea of an almost-rhythmic pattern of interludes, Schlesinger did not estimate the book as seriously as other critics—Moynahan, O'Malley, Rank—but he did consider it as successful within its own limits: "As before, O'Connor's young women are perfunctory. But his men (and his old cronies), his sense of family, his sense of confrontation, and the wit and zest of the dialogue are, as always, limpid and uproarious."

In brief, every aspect of the book tended to polarize the critics. Some saw the story as a loose sequence of vaudeville acts; others, as a tight, intense, psychological drama. Daniel was seen as "outrageously vital" and as a "wearisome mediocrity." The cronies were either dismissed as "docile stooges" or praised as a "delicately stylized chorus." While no one complained about any lack of talk, there was disagreement as to whether the dialogues were superfluous, repetitious, and boring, or whether they were valid and functional—individually, in adding elements of plot and characterization; cumulatively, in switching the audience's allegiance away from Daniel.

Tom was seldom noticed or mentioned by the reviewers, although this is as much *his* story as Daniel's. Daniel is a "fixed" character with no inner conflict; he is simply determined to stay. The obvious, spectacular part of the novel is the presentation of his tactical maneuvers against an external opponent. Yet, at the same time as this noisy entertainment achieves the center of attention, a quiet, subtle inner conflict is being developed in Tom's presentation. Tom is, at first, passive and inert about his father's presence in the house: "he preferred solutions that came without his direct intervention." Then he is moved by his wife to serve the eviction notice, wavers after talking to Brother Martin, and is pressured again by his wife; increasingly, he is disturbed by guilt, by his sense of debt and duty and obligation to his father, and by his father's appeal as a charming rogue. All of this internal conflict occurs *before* the final confrontation scene which is so loaded with the nuances of Tom's inner conflict that it cannot be briefly summarized.

I Was Dancing apparently can be read by some as a delightful entertainment, but readers looking for "escape literature" are warned that they ought to skim quickly through the final chapter or be prepared to get something more than they bargained for. As an account of a "game," the intricate maneuvers demand the reader's full attention. Read as an archetypal conflict between father and son, the novel is highly provocative; the ambiguities are built in. Both Daniel and Tom are disturbing characters; neither can be neatly catalogued because each one's actions and attitudes evoke such a multiplicity of responses. Although this book lacks the scope suggested by other O'Connor novels, the intensity of the focus is a significant compensation. As Michael O'Malley said, "Edwin O'Connor has turned now to that small place where the knives are sharper and the bleeding more prolonged: the family." *I Was Dancing* has been vastly underrated, generally unnoticed . . . but worth reading.

CHAPTER 9

All in the Family

I *Background*

FOR readers today, it is difficult to divorce the phrase "All in the Family" from our images and memories of Archie Bunker and that famous television series of the early 1970's. But here is another case of coincidence and circumstance: although Atlantic-Little, Brown protested when the name of that television series was first announced, no one at that time realized the eventual popularity and impact of that controversial series. Thus, today's reader of O'Connor's novel inevitably associates the phrase with Archie Bunker. Prior to that television series, however, coincidence and circumstance linked O'Connor's novel very tightly with the Kennedy family. Within this chapter, the reader should be able to make a more accurate assessment of this relationship.

All in the Family (1964) seems to reflect several of O'Connor's personal interests and memories. His friends have suggested that his marriage and subsequent family life gave him a new sense of fulfillment; and perhaps this development acounts for his attempt in this novel, for the first time, to depict *married couples*. Children also appear more frequently in his later works, and their doing so may have been caused by his new awareness of children as O'Connor attempted to be a good father to his step-son, Stephen, during the boy's maturing years (10–16). In addition, the intensely lyrical writing in the early part of *All in the Family* in which the narrator, as a boy, travels alone with his father in Ireland might be an imaginative fusion of the memories of two pleasant adventures in O'Connor's own past: his boyhood trip to California alone with his father, and his two restful vacations in Ireland.

The novel is dedicated to Arthur Thornhill, Sr., Chairman of the Board at Little, Brown. Thornhill, a unique "self-made" man, had started working at the publishing company in 1913 as a shipping clerk, and had worked his way up to the presidency by 1948. Combining business acumen with a humane attitude, Thornhill was responsible for much of the unusual growth of the company under his leadership. But to Edwin O'Connor, as well as to other writers such as John Marquand, Lillian Hellman, Erskine Caldwell, and Walter Edmonds, Thornhill was more than a business associate. To O'Connor especially, Thornhill represented a source of wisdom, a special kind of friendship with an older man. As one of their associates said: "A father-son relationship might sound too saccharine . . . more like a favorite uncle, someone with whom you could disagree without the problems of filial respect. Both men had a mutual admiration for each other's professional capacities." Although the novel is dedicated to Thornhill, it is important to note that the publisher satirized within the novel is *not* based on Thornhill.

O'Connor was in the midst of writing *All in the Family* when President Kennedy was assassinated; to O'Connor, the death was a traumatic experience. He had, after all, closer ties than most people to the Kennedy family, having known both the older brothers, John and Robert, from personal association in Boston and Cape Cod. Although O'Connor was not an intimate, the Kennedy circle was open to him because of the many mutual friends. Considering that O'Connor had been deeply involved in thinking and writing about the changing generations of the Irish family, the critic should reflect on this fact, plus O'Connor's own reputation for integrity, before charging that this novel was a commercial exploitation of the Kennedy tragedy. But, in fact, these charges were made; they are discussed after the novel itself has been examined. As an effective antidote to the pre-conceptions that many readers have that *All in the Family* is "about" the Kennedys (and thus waste their time trying to find the "key," to equate the various Kinsella brothers with the Kennedy brothers), two other ideas are suggested as more reasonable "pre-conceptions": if readers are going to give special attention to something, they will be much more rewarded by thinking about *the family* and by closely watching *the narrator*.

First, although the American "family novel" has its roots far back in our literary history (James Fenimore Cooper, William Dean Howells, Henry James, Theodore Dreiser, Willa Cather,

Edith Wharton), the exploration of conflicts within the family seems to have received more attention in recent years. The families in the fiction of William Faulkner, J. D. Salinger, Saul Bellow, John Updike, John O'Hara, Truman Capote, Carson Mc-Cullers, James Baldwin, William Styron, and Flannery O'Connor immediately come to mind, as well as the family conflicts drama-tized by Eugene O'Neill, Tennessee Williams, and Arthur Miller. And certainly scores of other writers—especially the one-book, semi-autobiographical confessors—fit easily into this category of the "family novel."

All of these recent literary expositions of the private griefs of the family should be placed in contrast to the *public* ideal of what the family should be. For one of the most strongly held myths in America, encouraged especially by the churches, has been that of the "holy family," an aggressionless group of people living together in domestic harmony and bliss. By promulgating this vision as a public "norm" for the family, the inevitable result has been that most people, witnessing the conflicts within their own families, conceal their "problem" from the outside world and anguish over the "failure" of their family life. This anguish has driven some to the psychiatrist's couch; some to the bottle; and some, it seems, to the typewriter to exorcise the old ghosts. "All of us are doomed," as Richard Schickel (in *Life*, October 30, 1970, 16) said, "in some way, to continue until our own deaths the dialogue with parents that began in forgotten childhood."

The fallacy of this "holy family" myth is that it denied the naturalness of human *aggression*. As Dr. George Bach noted, in *The Intimate Enemy:* "Spokesmen for the Judeo-Christian re-ligions have urged people to pray it away. Psychiatrists have tried to analyze it or rationalize it away. The late Emily Post and other etiquette devotees would have liked to smile it away. Nothing has worked and for the most logical reason. Anger is a part of the personality, like the sex drive. It can be displaced, channeled, modified, or repressed. But it cannot go away." But this kind of realistic acknowledgment of human aggressive instincts was not generally a part of Edwin O'Connor's generation. It was to come a little later; as Richard Hofstader said in the "Introduction" to *American Violence* (1970): "The rediscovery of our violence will undoubtedly be one of the most important intellectual legacies of the 1960s."

O'Connor matured in that post-World War II generation of veterans returning to an America in which the "holy family" myth was most intense. In this era, "togetherness" was preached as the ideal and attainable goal. Millions of veterans and their wives moved to the newly built suburbs, those jerry-built Arcadias; and the "baby boom" was on. Big, happy families became the ideal; even Hollywood sanctioned the urge by concurring that it was "Cheaper by the Dozen" and "The More the Merrier." While such "togetherness" was influential in the secular and non-Catholic spheres, it was positively mandatory within the Catholic community. There, "the family that prayed together, stayed together"; and Catholic-Mother-of-the-Year awards were distributed liberally to mothers of eight or more. In this pre-Pill era, the heyday of the "holy family," fecundity was equated with sanctity. As a corollary to the fertile mother, the image of the benevolent despot, the authoritarian father, existed. "Father knows best" had a dual implication—for both the home and the local parish. There was nothing wrong with the old traditional family structure as long as everyone involved "knew his place" and was contented with it: father as benevolent despot; mother as contented slave (idealized as "head and heart" of the family); children as docile, obedient team-members. But millions of Americans were being *displaced* in this era as the old certitudes were crumbling. Catholics especially, because they had been long sheltered in a hierarchical religious structure and educated in a disciplinarian school system, were ripe for an extreme cultural shock of displacement as their seemingly solid edifice began to show the cracks.

Looking backward now on the public image of the "holy family," one can probably say that its advocates did protest too much. Such an overemphasis on the virtues of the wholesome, happy family only suggest now that the public *assertions* of this ideal were, in reality, desperate *appeals*. Because, in fact, the traditional family structure for most Americans was under severe stress and strain. The "extended family" was disintegrating; the "nuclear family" was emerging. The new suburbs meant the breakdown of the old ghetto. The G.I. Bill meant a college degree for millions of veterans who came from homes where parents had stopped their schooling at an early age; the resultant tensions here are described by Hofstader in *Anti-Intellectualism in Amer-*

ican Life. When babies came along, they were apt to be reared by anxious parents holding *Doctor Spock's Baby Book*, that Bible of Suburbia, in their hands. Spock's "permissiveness," which was later blamed for all the "evils" of that crop of children, was essentially anti-authoritarian in that he advocated treating children as if they were human beings with individual rights, not simply inferior members of a hierarchy. Many other factors (soaring divorce rates, imposed job mobility, and commuting) were also working against the stability of the family; no wonder that "togetherness" was preached so often. This *milieu* is that of O'Connor's generation, which he reflects in *All in the Family* as the younger people, in this Americanization process, depart from the traditions of their elders. As it is, *All in the Family* is a stark parable that the "holy family" myth isn't true. In this, O'Connor joins other novelists and dramatists of the era who recognized and rendered the painful realities of family life and the human situation.

Second, one ought to read this novel by paying very close attention to the narrator, Jack Kinsella, because he is the filter through which the reader sees the story. Very few scenes are dramatized; most of the book is told from the narrator's recollections, with his own selection, deletion, emphasis. The story is his, his own experience of an *epiphany*—a new awareness—which he gains as he witnesses the catastrophe of a family. For the narrator, the crucial action is not so much a direct conflict, like the confrontation within Uncle Jimmy's family, as it is a movement from ignorance to knowledge. O'Connor's narrative technique is basically comparable to that in *The Edge of Sadness,* but in *All in the Family* there is no "disclaimer" by the narrator at the beginning. Jack Kinsella simply begins by telling one story, then another, then another.

II *The Novel*

All in the Family opens with two foreshadowings—of the narrator's boyhood trip to Ireland alone with his father, and of an unnamed family tragedy. But, once introduced, this ominous or tragic theme is dropped while the narrator, Jack Kinsella, recalls his "happy" family life during his boyhood. Recollected fragments reveal the idyllic experiences of growing up content and comfortable as a child in a rich family. Although his parents are frequently absent, when they are home they give Jack and his younger brother their full attention. In the interim, the children are reared by two loving caretakers. Jack's mother, an actress and singer before her marriage, prefers the city life and her actor friends, but she dutifully accompanies her husband and children to their favorite cabin at a wooded lakeside. There she worries about the boats tipping over because she fears drowning, but Jack's father demonstrates his rugged versatility in these scenes at the cabin.

Three brief episodes, which are related by theme, close the opening section of the novel. As Jack recalls his father's inventive bedtime stories, his mother's theatrical friends, and his father's magic tricks, the underlying emphasis is on the illusion-reality theme. The boy is innocent and ignorant; the narration is limited to the boy's viewpoint. He neither comprehends the subtle father-mother communication during the storytelling, nor can discern the illusions created by the performers in the family theatricals.

In contrast to the opening montage of many childhood memories, the last part of the chapter focuses on one event, the tragedy. The transition, appropriately, is abrupt and shocking. Vacationing at the cabin, the family is delighted by an unseasonably warm spring morning. Jack and his father are working, patching cement, when the mother appears in her bathing suit, inviting them to join her for a canoe ride. Jack and his father decline, but the six-year-old brother goes along. Replying to the father's farewell, the mother waves and says, "We may surprise you: we may never come back!" The narrator reports only his own reaction here: "And as she called this out to us, her voice was light and very gay. It was almost as if she were singing." (Later, the reader might interpret this as a sign of hysteria, and wonder about the father's reaction, or lack of action, at this moment.) Father and son continue working until they hear a shout a few minutes later; running to the lake, they see the canoe, empty and upright. Frantically, they row out in a leaky rowboat; and, as they search the deep water, Jack tells of his own feelings then: "suddenly I had the terrible feeling that at any moment he might topple overboard and get lost like my mother and Tom, and in that case what would become of me?"

As the narrator describes his father's actions, diving and searching for the bodies, it is apparent that Jack's strongest memories are of his own egocentric fears: "I was so frightened by my own danger that I could think of absolutely nothing else. . . . I completely forgot the reason, the terrible reason, for our being out on the lake in the first place. I did not once think of my mother or of Tom." As Jack relates the rest of the details of that day's search, the emphasis remains on his egocentric fears and feelings. A summary narrative of the funeral details and a transition to the Ireland trip close this opening chapter. Three times within this chapter, allusions have been made to Uncle Jimmy; these are minor remarks, seemingly irrelevant, but should be noted because they substantiate the subtle structural links within the novel.

Chapter Two opens and closes with attention given to Uncle Jimmy, but the two main scenes within the chapter are set in the hotel and on the walking tour of Dublin. Again the illusion-reality theme is prominent as all of the father's grand promises about sightseeing never materialize; and Jack, almost neutrally, notes this fact: "The funny thing was that when he did get to Ireland, none of these things my father talked about ever really happened." At the hotel, they meet Lord Ivermorris, a grotesque old man; and Jack's illusions about nobility (drawn from Medieval romances) are completely shattered. Mr. Guilfoyle, the hotel manager, is a "stage Irishman"; but, in reality, Guilfoyle's mannerisms are ironic, a mockery of the stereotype which Americans have of the Irish. The only time in *all* of O'Connor's writings that the "Irish" clichés ("Mother Machree and the Rose of Tralee") are used, the gross exaggeration indicates that Guilfoyle is mocking his own "tourist act" for the benefit of Jack's father. Here it is revealed that this is the same hotel where Jack's parents spent their honeymoon years ago; to Jack, the hotel is "most elegant," but his father sees it as "getting a little shabby." Jack does not comprehend his father's nostalgic trance during this interlude in the hotel or on their walking tours of Dublin visiting the spots where his parents had walked years ago.

Chapter Three takes father and son through the Irish countryside to visit the castle of Uncle Jimmy. To provide background for the boy, who knows little about his father's older brother, the father sketches the family history as they drive through the pastoral landscape. The boy's great-grandfather had come to

America as a railroad laborer; his son had run away from home early, worked as a seaman, speculated in California real estate, and built a fortune in land and banking before returning to the East where he married and settled down to raise three children: Uncle Jimmy, Gert, and Jack's father. Uncle Jimmy was the favorite son, and he had his father's rapacious instinct for making money. Jack's father then justifies his own attitude toward money, as a *means* instead of a goal, in contrast to Uncle Jimmy's attitude. In the talk of money throughout this book, the reader may feel that O'Connor is working out his own credo concerning it; he is coping with his own sudden fortune after *The Last Hurrah* by defining the "proper attitude."

Arriving at Uncle Jimmy's castle, Jack discovers that it is a genuine Medieval fortress; but, bleak and dowdy, it is nothing like the imagined spendor he had anticipated; unfit for habitation, the castle's actual living quarters are in an adjacent, more modern building. Uncle Jimmy and his three sons meet the visitors, and the first thing Jack notices is the fierceness of Uncle Jimmy and the roughness of the easy-going banter among his three cousins: James, fourteen, the sophisticate who smokes and drinks tea; Phil, eleven, Jack's own age; and Charles, nine, the babyish show-off.

The following scene centers on the boys at play and their boyhood relationships. Jack admires James for his suave, confidant gracefulness; Charles, the youngest, frantically tries to keep up with the older boys and constantly seeks their approval; Phil becomes Jack's best friend, the intimate sharer of confidences. The boys play no Irish games, nor do they have Irish friends. They live in a self-contained world, even having a tutor instead of going to a school. (This isolation may help to explain the *delayed* maturation and the explosive disintegration of this family later; a more typical family experiences peer-group and school influences early.) Jack emphasizes the tight family spirit of his three cousins: "Among themselves they argued as much as anybody, but this was all in the family; whenever anything outside the family came up they were all very loyal to each other and always stuck together." This observation ironically foreshadows the climax so strongly that it is difficult to understand those critics who dismiss the boyhood memories as being unrelated to the later political story.

Later, when Jack is shocked by Uncle Jimmy's fierce hollering and rough slapping of his sons for their minor disobediences, the cousins defend their father's rough actions as signs of his love and pride in them. When Jack says that he has never been hit by *his* father, Phil sincerely warns him that he might grow up to be a "slob." This contrast between types of fathers and families is repeated in the next major scene in which Jack's father argues with Uncle Jimmy, and this juxtaposition forms an important theme in the novel as the narrator observes the authoritarian father and his three sons. When Phil asks more about Jack's family life, Jack's innocent, simple version of the drowning is one that can never be recaptured after he has overheard his father's version.

That night, listening at a heat vent upstairs, Jack overhears an argument between his father and Uncle Jimmy. Uncle Jimmy sees himself as "head of the family" and attempts to persuade Jack's father to leave the boy in his care so that Jack will grow up with his cousins. Jack's father rejects this offer, affirms his love for his son, and argues bitterly with his brother about their own father. Uncle Jimmy, defending his father, denounces his brother as a parasite who lacks family spirit. Jack's father savagely argues against his brother by describing their own father as a tyrannical miser; any family money he received from the old man, Jack's father felt, was simply restitution, "war damages," for the harm inflicted on himself and on his mother who was "kept in her place" in the kitchen scrubbing floors when they could have afforded a maid. When Jack's father attacks Uncle Jimmy's "romantic notion" of a family dynasty, Uncle Jimmy's counterattack diverts this argument by asking Jack's father what is really wrong with him and what happened at the drowning.

Unaware of the boy listening upstairs, Jack's father reveals his own anxieties and doubts about the drowning. Jack's father relates that the canoe was *dry* and tells of his delayed realization of the implications of this fact. Fragments of conversation about his wife's "ups and downs" suggest her mental instability, but Jack's father says that, at the time of the incident, that "there wasn't a trace, not even a hint . . . if there had been, naturally I wouldn't have let her go." When he remarks that he had even suggested that she go out on the lake that day, he proclaims his own guilt. But Uncle Jimmy comforts him by saying that any speculations as to the drowning as not being purely accidental are unfounded; they are caused by natural reactions to grief.

Uncle Jimmy asks whether the boy, Jack, was aware of his mother's illness. Jack's father replies that it was concealed from the children by the pretext of taking long trips whenever her bad moods were anticipated; *but, he repeats again, his wife had given no warning this time.* Speculating on the possibilities about his wife's death, Jack's father concludes with a cry that he should have stopped her. Uncle Jimmy comforts him as the conversation ends.

The shattering effect of this overheard conversation is evident in the next scene in which Jack is unable to make sense of the fragments. Disturbed and trembling, he plans to remember everything he heard so that some day he could understand. The remark about the dry canoe doesn't make sense to him, nor does the account of the mother being sick. The boy's innocence, his unawareness of appearance—reality differences, had been previously established; this scene marks the awful beginning of knowledge. The chapter ends with a brief transitional scene in which Jack and his father prepare to leave Ireland. The close friendship with Phil is emphasized as the two boys scrawl out "A Pact between THE FIERCE AND FRIENDLY TWO," promising to stay friends all of their lives, to see each other often, and to revenge any harms the other sustains. A month after Jack returns to America, he is sent to boarding school; and his boyhood is ended.

Book One is undeniably Jack's story. In the remainder of the novel, the surface action (the political story) narrated by Jack probably gets the most attention from the reader. But the seeds of the inner drama of Jack's life have already been planted in these opening recollections of boyhood memories: the family, the father-son relationships the innocence-experience theme, the illusion-reality theme, love and loss.

Book Two (chapters 4, 5, 6) occurs many years afterwards, just after Charles, the youngest of the cousins, has been elected governor of the state. The background is filled in as Jack prepares (Chapter 4) to go to the large, public victory celebration (Chapter 5); afterwards, he is invited to the private family gathering (Chapter 6). The narrator's role as a "neutral inside-observer" is established; like Adam Caufield in *The Last Hurrah,* Jack has family ties to the political leader, but he has no partisan involve-

ment and has been long absent from the city. Jack had once,
briefly, been Frank Skeffington's secretary during that mayor's
last campaign, but his disillusioning experience at city hall—"that
shabby, sordid, hilarious place"—had left him apolitical. (This
link suggests that O'Connor was now consciously thinking in
terms of an *interrelated* saga of the Irish-American experience.)

Chapter 4 opens with a description of Charles' gubernatorial
campaign, a sophisticated television blitz managed by outside
experts, which created the image of "sincerity" and managed to
conceal the aloof coldness which Charles has in person. Charles'
main assets for the governor's job are his wealth, his attractive
wife, his four years as the mayor of the city, and, with insiders,
his reputation for ruthless manipulation. A flashback to a period
five years earlier tells of Charles' decision to enter politics because
Uncle Jimmy had decided it was the family's duty. The eldest
son, James, was ineligible (revealed later); and Phil, the idealist,
estimated that Charles had a better chance of winning. Phil is
content to be the unobtrusive manager, the unseen aide, in the
good cause of reform politics. The narrator emphasizes that Phil
and Charles look like twins, in externals almost identical; thus
as *foil* characters, these brothers underline the appearance-reality
theme.

Chapter 5 is the crowd scene, the kaleidoscopic set of impres-
sions of the people at the victory celebration. As Jack tours the
crowded reception, he meets Edso and Walshie, two "comic
grotesques" from Skeffington's era who function as a transition
device to compare the *old* homogeneous political rallies with the
new heterogeneous collection of odd political bedfellows. With
a good ear for mimicry, O'Connor moves his narrator through
the crowd as he overhears fragments of talk from "jet-set" name-
droppers, parlor psychiatrists, Catholic chauvinists, academic
bores, labor union toughs, and mealy-mouthed intellectuals. In
brief, Jack states, it is "a gathering of disparate social, racial, and
intellectual forces which would have been unthinkable" in the
old days.

Jack meets Marie, Charles' attractive wife; and, as they talk,
Jack's own situation is obliquely revealed. He is now a successful, popular novelist, a writer of "suspense" stories; and there is
a foreshadowing of his own domestic problem, his separation
from his wife, Jean. After Marie leaves, Jack meets Charles; and

the men discuss politics. Jack recalls the extensive history of corruption, almost unique to that city and state, which makes it so hard to be an honest politician. Memories of Skeffington are strong in this section; Charles, as if to show Jack that Skeffington's ability can be matched, uses a Skeffington trick to steer a boring VFW Commander to Jack; and Jack uses a Skeffington trick to endure this conversation: he gives the *appearance* of listening without really paying attention to the man. Jack muses on Skeffington's skill in such deceptions; then he goes upstairs to join the private, family gathering in the library.

Although the transitional blends are smooth and unobtrusive between scenes, Chapter 6, the longest (67 pp.) in the book, is structured in eight recognizable scenes. An opening panorama surveys the family members gathered in the library: the gruff patriarch Uncle Jimmy; his sister, Gert; Phil Kinsella and his shy wife, Flossie; Marie, Charles' wife; and James, the eldest son, who is depicted as a sophisticated, worldly cleric. Charles, the governor, enters, having just returned from talking with the entrenched political boss of the state. The narrator is aware of the tension between Charles and his idealistic brother, Phil, about this contact with corruption. Counterpointed to the increasing split between the brothers, Uncle Jimmy begins to dominate the scene with his talk about family unity. As Uncle Jimmy continues to relate anecdotes about events in the past, the narrator speculates about the difference between how he had heard the same stories from his own father but in totally different versions. Jack is puzzled over the truth of these "separate accounts" and is unsettled by doubts as he recaps the uncertainties of the evening's conversations. He senses that something is wrong, but the *appearance* of family unity and cohesiveness reassures him.

With Skeffington as their main topic, Charles and Jack have a lengthy discussion about the old and the new politics; interwoven with this conversation is the idea of change within the family. But, as Charles leaves, he affirms his own "sense of family" and remarks, hesitatingly, about his brother's aid: "Phil is . . . my conscience, I suppose. Or so it appears." Uncle Jimmy again dominates the next scene; the emphasis is first on his disappointment with his eldest son, James, for becoming a priest, but the focus then shifts to Uncle Jimmy's disappointment with Phil. Phil, a competent lawyer with great potential, is dissatisfied with his life which seems to him to be an absurd pursuit of trivialities. Uncle Jimmy is exasperated with Phil's restlessness, unsympathetic with his idealism; however, when Charles had decided to run for office five years earlier, Phil had dedicated himself to this mission of reform politics, for he has a "vision of what could be done if the right person was in power." In the next scene, Jack talks with Phil and gets his view of the political situation. Phil is enthusiastic that the old corrupt politicians have lost their *power* because of Charles' election: "they don't have control any more. *We* have that." As they talk, Jack notices that Charles is now speaking with some of the corrupt politicians; but Phil dismisses his doing so as merely a show of party unity. However, Jack is aware that something is wrong.

In the final scenes, the emphasis returns to Jack's personal life and his past memories. In oblique fragments throughout this chapter, hints and foreshadowings have prepared the way for the revelation of Jack's separation from his wife, Jean. When Jack returns to his empty house that evening, Jean calls on the phone, contrite, asking to come back to him. Neither the cause of their split nor the full meaning of the conversation is revealed here, a transitional link to Book Three (chapters 7 and 8) in which the "domestic" plot emerges as Jean returns to the family: the private talk with Jack (Chapter 7), and the more public reunion with the Kinsella clan at the Inaugural Ball (Chapter 8).

Chapter 7 takes place at Phil and Flossie's isolated beach house in Georgia where Jack and Jean have joined them for a brief midwinter vacation. The opening scene furthers the characterization of Phil and Flossie, emphasizing their strong moral sense of values and establishing credibility for Flossie's outburst later in the story. However, most of the chapter is in the narrator's account of the private reconciliation between himself and his wife. As Jean tells Jack why she had deserted him, why she had an affair with another man and had fled to Europe, Jack describes his response in terms of disbelief and incomprehension: "baffled," "stupefied," "badly confused." Jean charges that Jack, who had been preoccupied with his work and with his own past, had treated her as a possession or a thing. Lonely, and childless, she sought for some attention. After telling about her affair and her "make believe" gaiety afterwards, Jean starts berating herself. Jack, desperate for her love, promises to do better, meditates about his own carelessness and culpability, and resolves a new tenderness.

Chapter 8 opens on Charles' inauguration day, with Jack's watching the ceremonies on television, noting Charles' "sincerity" image, and the ironies of the coverage that juxtaposes onstage rhetoric with the visual shots of the bizarre politicians in the audience. The main action of the chapter, however, occurs at the Inaugural Ball that evening and centers on anxieties and awkwardness of the situation as Jean "rejoins" the family. Uncle Jimmy's reaction is crucial: when the old patriarch accepts her, the tension is broken. The final paragraph foreshadows danger as Jack notes that the evening's joy and warmth and family unity would not occur again.

Book Four (chapters 9 and 10) shows how the new political situation of the Kinsella family impinges on Jack's personal life, as outsiders seek favors (Chapter 9) and as he gets involved in the family's problem (Chapter 10). Book Four opens with an increased distance and separation from the family as everyone is extremely busy with his own affairs, but it closes with Jack's return from Europe to get involved in the family conflict. In Chapter 9, Jack observes pressure groups (Mrs. Elderberry) seeking political favors, and he is involved when his obsequious publisher (Andrew Post) seeks his influence with Charles. Jack's own writing has bogged down; he and Jean plan a second honeymoon to Ireland to mend their own lives. Farewell visits by Marie and Phil repeat the themes of Jean's childlessness and the impending family disaster.

Chapter 10 summarizes Jack and Jean's six-month vacation. Instead of Ireland, they socialize in London until Jack gets disturbed about his lack of writing. Searching for a haven, they relax in an old hotel in Florence, Italy, where Jack works well in an idyllic retreat from trouble. (A "comic grotesque" character, Signor Barbettura, here underlines the appearance-reality theme.) Eventually, letters from home, telling of Phil's increased symptoms of alienation and withdrawal, cause Jack's decision to return to help Phil. Leaving Florence, Jack comments "I had never been so happy in all my life," a statement echoing his remark three hundred pages earlier, immediately before the idyllic family life of his boyhood was shattered.

Book Five (chapters 11, 12, 13, 14) presents Phil's side of the political argument (Chapter 11) and also Charles' (Chapter 12); moves toward the confrontation and climax of this conflict (Chapter 13); and then, in the denouement (Chapter 14) interweaves the other plots (boyhood memories, domestic split) to focus back on Jack's personal life.

Phil's version of the family's trouble begins with some seemingly rambling anecdotes, but these stories are all centered on corruption and deceitful appearances (Judge Kilrane) as a prelude to his charge that Charles is becoming corrupt. Phil concedes that Charles has been a reasonably good governor and is likely to view Phil as a "perfectionist," but Charles has not even attempted to root out the entrenched corrupt politicians. Charles, Phil claims, has fallen in love with politics and power. Phil thinks that Charles has a tacit truce with the old politicians; in return for not disturbing the *status quo*, Charles has made some highly visible achievements with their cooperation that will enable him to use his office as a springboard to national politics. Phil claims that Charles has the *power* to destroy local corruption, but the fight would be bitter and complex, harmful perhaps to Charles' new personal ambitions of becoming a senator. Phil flatly declares that he is going to stop Charles and that he has told his brother of his plan to make a public exposure of local corruption unless Charles begins to reform. To Phil, Jack's reaction is unexpected when he argues against this plan as being a senseless destruction of the family over a rather common political disagreement about what strategy or means can be used to achieve a goal. When Jack begs Phil to come out of his "Dostoievsky dream," Phil argues more heatedly, voice raised and body shaking, with a "queer light" in his eyes, "a strange unsettled look."

Chapter 12 presents Charles' side of the argument as the governor defends his pragmatic position that he has to work with the men available—good, bad, or indifferent—simply to make the state operate. Charles claims that Phil wants to lead a "moral crusade" and has issued an ultimatum to do things his way. Charles, sensing the unreality of Phil's idealistic proposals, has had to assert his own independent judgment. Jack is almost persuaded by Charles' reasonable explanation of the allegations, but he suddenly becomes skeptical of the governor's "sheer believability"— that image of absolute candor which Jack had previously witnessed on television. Then Jack abruptly asks Charles if he is planning to run for the Senate, "And with this one, single, unpre-meditated question, everything came apart." Caught off guard, Charles assumes "an absolute neutrality of expression," a carefully controlled mask which Jack knows is a lie: "in that same instant I knew that whatever its strangeness—or his strangeness—Phil's version was the truth!"

While a bare summary might suggest a melodrama (Realist versus Idealist), the narrator's intricate reactions to the ambigu-ities of Phil's sanity and Charles' motives deserve close attention. After Charles closes the conversation with a vague threat against Phil, Uncle Jimmy, who has been a silent observer during the talk, rages against Phil's disloyalty. Later, the old man telephones Jack to apologize for this outburst; as Uncle Jimmy reveals his own confusion, Jack sees the anguish of the old patriarch who is now completely powerless despite his nominal leadership as "father of the family . . . boss of the tribe."

The final confrontation begins in Chapter 13 when Phil writes a sarcastic "Letter to the Editor," signed "Edmund Burke," in which he criticizes one of the governor's recent judicial appoint-ments. Phil, who had forewarned Charles of this opening salvo, had ignored Charles' request not to do it. Two days later, Phil's wife hysterically calls Jack to tell him that Phil has been served with legal papers ordering his commitment to a mental institution. At this news, Jack is stunned, immobilized with the catastrophe of the situation. He describes his feelings in terms which link all three major plots in the novel: "It was the kind of moment I'd had just twice before in my life: the first time when I was a little boy and had at last realized that I would never see my mother again; the second . . . when I learned that Jean had left me. In rare and terrible moments like these I think a small annihilation takes place, so that a part of you is burned away and never quite comes back. . . ."

Thus, the boyhood tragedy, the domestic separation, and the conflict within the Kinsella family are finally fused together; and while not directly related to one another, they all directly relate to the narrator's most intense experiences of love and loss. For readers concerned with the *coherence* of the novel's structure, who have been anticipating *how* and *when* O'Connor would tie his divergent stories together, this scene is a tactician's delight, a fulfillment not commonly found. The closer the reader gets to the end of the novel, the more imperative it becomes that these themes must fuse. If O'Connor, like his novelist-narrator here, is writing a "suspense" story, he has maintained it for nearly four hundred pages, a most ambitious extension of his "detour" style. Edmund Wilson (in the "Baldini" memoir) notes that "the unexplained suicide of the narrator's mother is echoed and balanced later by the unfaithfulness and flight of his wife"; here, it is clear that both of these earlier catastrophes are linked in the narrator's feelings with the obvious surface story of Phil's commitment.

As Jack meditates about the possibility of Phil's being railroaded to a mental institution, the insanity theme again merges the boyhood tragedy with the present moment: "I think I was troubled most of all by a vague persisting fear of the word 'madness' itself, applied to someone who was close to me, whom I had known so well. This was an old terror of mine; it came and went; it began I suppose in my childhood, when I didn't yet understand what it was, but knew that it had already played a part in my life." Jack recalls his lifelong suspicion about his mother's condition and that he was never able to ask his father about it until his father's dying moments: "not even then quite asking the question. 'About Mom . . .' I didn't complete it, and my father looked back at me for a long time: in our lives together we had never talked about this. Then he said simply, 'I don't know, Jack. I never knew'." Thus the narrator (and the reader) is left with the ambiguities unresolved. Jack is unable to find certitude; certain aspects (including whether his father heard the mother's parting remark) will always remain a mystery. Mrs. Yntema, O'Connor's editor, recalled later (in an interview with me) that she had discussed this ambiguity with O'Connor:

Ed would never call it suicide. He wanted to leave it ambiguous as to whether it was suicide or an accident or what. And I think that the mother as really being mad was something that he never quite said to himself; he never went all of the way in saying that she was mad. He never said whether the mother drowned the little boy on purpose, dragged him out of the boat with her. I did ask him that, but he just didn't want to say. I never called it "suicide" when I talked to him because he preferred the word "disappearance." He wanted to leave it a little ambiguous. It's more terrifying that way, I think.

The Kinsella clan gathers at Charles' house for the climactic argument. Charles had arranged for the secret medical certification, and the legal work is going to be "fixed" by the corrupt Judge Kilrane. As Phil is describing what he considers to be a frame-up, Jack's reactions focus on his own impotency, again in terms of his personal griefs: "It was like being a spectator at a drowning: a helpless spectator, unable in any way to prevent the tragedy that was to come, and yet at the same time feeling that this tragedy need not come if only one of the other spectators— a particular one—would merely raise his voice or lift a finger." (The direct reference is to Uncle Jimmy, but indirectly it may suggest Jack's father's inaction when his wife made her strange farewell remark.)

Charles argues that the commitment is not a frame-up; regrettably, he says, Phil *is obsessed* with unrealistic ideas. When Phil seeks Uncle Jimmy's intervention, the old man denounces both Phil and James (the priest) as traitors to the family. Phil's shy wife responds with a very bitter outburst against the old man as a "dreadful, horrible, insensitive, vulgar, stupid little tyrant!" Then Phil reveals his counterattack: he will promise to stop his attacks against Charles. At first, Jack thinks this a surrender, not understanding the implications of Phil's promise. Then Phil explains that he has put Charles in the position of choosing between the "safe" way (destroying Phil's public credibility by temporary confinement and official certification of "mental instability") and the "risk" of trusting his brother's word. Phil sees his "trust" proposal as a last-ditch effort to shock Charles into recognizing that personal ambition is destroying his character.

As the gathering breaks up, Jack assures Phil of his sympathy and friendship; Phil responds by quoting from memory their boyhood friendship pact. As Phil leaves, Uncle Jimmy cries out: "What the hell has happened to my family?" This dramatic understatement, set in context of the long, complicated argument, is quite effective—a memorable synopsis of a family tragedy. Jack realizes that they were "as a family finished forever."

The final chapter begins with the simple statement that Phil was committed three days later. The narrator is limited in knowing the details of the family's affairs as his contact with them is now so slight. After a dreary interval, Jean suggests that they visit Ireland; their previously planned "second honeymoon" never did materialize. Before they leave, they are visited by Aunt Gert who speaks about the family fight; and Jack is surprised by her matter-of-fact attitude. She calmly estimates that Phil will endure, reserving her sympathy for Uncle Jimmy as the most serious loser in this family catastrophe:

He's old and he's got nobody now. He's lost all his boys. He spent all his life bringing them up and hoping they'd all be just like him. That's what he wanted: a house full of little Jimmies. Well, it didn't turn out that way, and anyone with half an eye could see it couldn't. First he lost James and now he's lost Phil, and the only one left is Charles. And he's really lost him too, only he doesn't know it yet. Oh, yes, it's very hard on Jimmy. Because he's all alone. And that can be hard on anybody. But most of all when you're someone like Jimmy who's had no practice at it.

As she leaves, Jack reflects that Aunt Gert is an extraordinary woman. And in an extraordinary passage O'Connor comes as close as possible, without writing an essay, to pointing out a "moral" in this stark parable: the tyrannical father destroys his own family. If this is O'Connor's thesis, it needs some serious qualifications. Certainly Uncle Jimmy's family has been destroyed, but it is because he *has* "a house full of little Jimmies." All three sons display varieties of authoritarianism: Charles, as the closest reproduction of his father, is on his way to usurping the old king's throne; James, the priest, is an "official" Father, but one who neglects his "family" because he is constantly absent. Finally, Phil's seemingly altruistic dreams of political reforms can be interpreted as a form of the "If-I-were-King" fantasy of power; in this case, the "If-I-were-Kingmaker," or "Power behind the Throne," is perhaps an inferiority-complex amendment to an authoritarian fantasy of power. (The narrator strongly sympathizes with Phil, but Jack is at least one step more detached from authoritarianism.)

After the Aunt Gert scene, the locale switches to Ireland where Jack and Jean are visiting in the old hotel. Memories of the past are stirred up by Mr. Guilfoyle and by Walshie, the old politician, who is also vacationing there. Oddly homesick, Jack does not want to return to America yet; but the couple does leave the hotel to move to a house in the Irish countryside, a pastoral haven which brings back happy memories of his boyhood trip with his father. Five quiet, happy months are spent here, filled with a new domestic joy and peace; Jack is working again, writing well on a new book. One day, Jean, unable to conceal her "triumphant happiness," tells Jack that she is pregnant; the long years of childlessness are over. Exuberantly, they make plans to return to America; they stop at Uncle Jimmy's castle to see him, but he is no longer there. The novel concludes: "And so, the next morning, I left Ireland again, to go back to the city I had always loved, to the house which had always been my home, but now, for the first time, with my dear Jean, to a family of my own."

Certainly the obvious interpretation of this new fatherhood suggests an optimism and a new hope for the future; Jack will have profited from his experience and his witness of the Kinsella family tragedy. O'Connor's friends recall that this book was a very difficult one for him to finish; he had been stalled, in several drafts, on the ending, but he eventually "sensed" this final version. His editor, Mrs. Yntema, later (in a letter to me) described O'Connor's creative problems with this ending:

The fatherhood at the end was not planned at the beginning. It was the one novel that he wrote that he admitted having trouble with. It was written and then he made some big revisions, more than I ever remember him doing. It was at that time that we rather pressed him to make more of a relationship with Jack Kinsella's wife, and he suddenly saw it and the title together. He realized what he was really talking about and built that up very strongly and then wound up with the pregnancy. The return to Ireland was in there from the beginning, as far as I know. The commitment of Phil was always planned.

III *Critical Response*

Readers in the future must remember that *All in the Family* was published in a period saturated with every conceivable kind of memorabilia of the late President Kennedy: plastic statues, photographs, trinkets. Literally hundreds of articles about Kennedy's life appeared in this era after his assassination. Although much of this outburst was genuinely motivated, fulfilling a real emotional need of the nation, there was also a concomitant commercial exploitation. Despite the fact that O'Connor was working on his own turf—the Irish, the family, politics—which he had demarcated long before, he encountered insinuations that he was another of those who were exploiting the tragedy of the Kennedys.

Robert Manning, editor of the *Atlantic*, recalled (in an interview with me) that O'Connor "was very conscious of the probability that no matter what the sources for this idea were that he was going to be accused of it being patterned on the Kennedy thing and I'm sure that he had been thinking about it a long time before that." Schlesinger, (p. 26) who was intimate with both Kennedy and O'Connor, described O'Connor's dilemma: "The reception of *All in the Family* was complicated by the insistence of reviewers on reading the novel as a *roman à clef* about the Kennedys. This prospect worried Ed a good deal as he worked on the book. But he could not see any way around it without discarding the idea entirely, and he was unwilling to let the fear of transitory journalistic scandal stop him from using a scheme he cared deeply about."

Half of the reviewers did suggest or imply that the novel was a *roman à clef* or some kind of exploitation of the Kennedys; the other half, although rejecting this idea, was certain to note that "other people" might make the claim. Eliot Fremont-Smith, in the *New York Times* of September 28, 1966, made the strongest insinuations as he claimed that O'Connor "tries to repeat the trick" pulled earlier in *The Last Hurrah*: "And once again Mr. O'Connor admits nothing, though 'everybody knows' that *All in the Family* is about the Kennedys. Only, of course, it isn't. One suspects that it just is meant to seem that way. The Kennedy name, even when not named, helps so many things, why not the sales of a novel?" This critic saw the novel as a paste-up of two separate stories, as if "O'Connor perhaps sensed that the Kennedy-inspired family story was not enough, so he added another plot about the narrator's marital problems" (45). Fremont-Smith did recognize the proportion given to the narrator; but, once this critic accepted the "Kennedy" premise, he concluded the "non-Kennedy" material was superfluous filler: "In fact, Jack Kinsella spends so much time remembering, observing, and being unaccountably sympathetic to all and sundry that it is a wonder that anything gets done at all. It is even questionable whether he recognizes the intended symmetry of the saga: as his immediate family flounders, Uncle Jimmy's coalesces; at the end, of course, it is vice-versa" (45). After this insight, Fremont-Smith returned to his major thesis that the novel was a benign fraud that exploited the public's curiosity and fascination with the Kennedy family.

Newsweek (September 19, 1966, 117A), *Library Journal* (July, 1966, 3471), and *Saturday Review* (October 1, 1966, 64) also emphasized the Kennedy idea, and Father R. F. Grady, in *Best Sellers* (October 1, 1966, 237), went so far as to describe the novel's "basic theme" as being "that one can with shrewd planning and the expenditure of large sums of money win political office." More discriminating reviewers spent less time on the Kennedy issue, but even these felt constrained to make some kind of opening apologia. Reading these reviews vividly illustrates how outside factors can influence the reception of a work. Just as the Joseph McCarthy issue overshadowed the reception of Arthur Miller's excellent play *The Crucible*, so did the aura of the Kennedys distract critical judgments about the intrinsic merit of *All in the Family*. Both cases presented difficult challenges to the reviewers.

After the critics had handled the Kennedy issue, some continued to discuss the novel itself. And the harshest criticism was "all in the family"—from Catholic periodicals—a group which is occasionally charged with parochial bias. Paul Cuneo, in *America* of October 1, 1966 (393), after suggesting that O'Connor's Pulitzer Prize was a consolation prize, described *All in the Family* as an overpriced, overlong, disjointed book which unsuccessfully merged "a limp, melodramatic political story" with "a limp, melodramatic romance." Gregor Roy, in *The Catholic World* of December, 1966 (180), after praising the opening section of the novel, itemized the defects in the rest: unreal characters, strained mood, stale wit, turgid drama, trite threadbare theme, banal female characters, and a re-hash of the earlier novels. In addition, Roy faulted the first-person narration (roughly equating Virtue with the Omniscient Narrator); and he declared that the "major theme" was "the old, attractively corrupt Tammany politicking versus the new, glossy but equally corrupt 'good image' politics." Robert Burns, in *The Critic* (October–November, 1966, 95), termed the book a bland "matinée performance" which neither unsettles nor involves the reader. O'Connor, he claims, has lost his punch, but should be able to continue to write salable novels which could be "turned into movie scripts." Once again, the old charges of commercialism are used; and the popular success of *The Last Hurrah* continued to haunt O'Connor.

Damning with faint praise, Arthur Darack, in *Saturday Review* of October 1, 1966 (64), placed the book "in that diversionary class of American novels that are earnest, blandly probing, gently cynical, and nostalgic." Darack saw its only novelty as being a patriarchal novel in an era of matriarchy. "Edwin O'Connor," he concluded, "is a kind of Faust of American ward politics; he does not truly believe in either the devil or redemption, though he believes in the reality of seduction through all its idioms." Here, it seems, is another echo of a familiar critical problem as the critic is uneasy with O'Connor's refusal to present a simplistic vision of good and evil.

The most enthusiastic reviews were those of Herbert Kenny, in the *New York Times Book Review* (September 25, 1966, 4), and of Howard Mumford Jones, in the *Atlantic* (October, 1966, 117–19), who had been invited to place the novel in a wider context in an extended essay-review, "Politics, Mr. O'Connor, and the Family Novel." The strength of Kenny's review is his close attention to the narrator as *filter* through which the story is told, thus emphasizing the importance of the narrator's inner awareness. Yet, Kenny felt unsatisfied at the end, desiring more resolutions: "In brief, O'Connor has committed himself to a chronicle. This novel . . . can only be appreciated in that light. Continued as ably, such a chronicle could assume a major place in American literature."

Howard Mumford Jones also emphasized the role of the narrator in the novel. Praising the opening boyhood section, which he said was "told through a Proustian feat of memory," Jones felt there was no "obvious preparation" with the Irish scenes for the later political story and that "one hunts about to see why this prologue to the main action exists." Here, Jones offered a twofold solution: "aside from the education of Jack through sorrow, we get these glimpses into the boyhood life of the three Kinsella lads as something like the natural environment of an Irish family. But the section also hints that the dislocation of Irish family life in America may be the remote cause of the final disaster." Then Jones, noting that O'Connor is often considered a political novelist, summarized the development of the American political novel as being divided generally into three phases. *The Last Hurrah* was placed in Jones' third category, those novels which stress the psychology of the politician; after lauding the "three-dimensional reality" of Skeffington and noting the political aspects of *All in the Family*, Jones argued that politics was "the occasion, not the theme" of the latter novel. O'Connor's main concern, Jones claimed, was "not the state, but the family."

Additionally, Jones, who pointed out O'Connor's "series of experiments in narrative by indirection," emphasized the cumulative force of the fragmented glimpses of Skeffington in *The Last Hurrah* and the sensitive narrative device in *The Edge of Sadness*. This indirect method of narration, Jones said, "is pushed to its limits in *All in the Family*. The first section has no apparent relation to the main narrative." Yet, the *real* major story is not on the surface, not about politics, but about the family. Jones concluded with a forceful judgment about O'Connor and his critics; speaking of the "long line of narrative achievement from Fielding through Scott and Dickens," Jones saw that "writers like O'Connor are proper heirs of the great tradition."

Edmund Wilson, in the preface to "The Great Baldini" fragment (in *The Best and the Last of Edwin O'Connor*), commented briefly on *All in the Family* noting that it portrayed the "Ivy League generation of Boston Irish" or "the Kennedy generation which stands somewhere between the old Irish world of Boston and the new world of cocktails and enlightenment." But Wilson, who dismissed the charges of a *roman à clef*, defended the imaginative powers of O'Connor and suggested that O'Connor was "evidently trying to deal, in a firm although underground way, with the sexual Puritanism of Irish Catholicism. The unexplained suicide of the narrator's mother is echoed and balanced later on by the unfaithfulness and flight of his wife—which, however, since times are changing, does not turn out to be equally serious, for the couple are later reunited."

After O'Connor's death, the poet Peter Davison, director of the Atlantic Monthly Press, summarized O'Connor's achievements. Writing in a local magazine (*Boston*, May, 1968, 61–62), Davison saw O'Connor as working in that branch of fiction "from Thackeray and Dickens . . . through the works of William Dean Howells, Sinclair Lewis, and F. Scott Fitzgerald." After praising O'Connor's ability with dialogue and characterization, Davison assessed *All in the Family* as O'Connor's best novel because of its balance, humanity, and variety.

Schlesinger's later evaluation (26) agreed: "Removed from the Kennedy connection and assessed in its own right, *All in the Family* must be considered, I think, his most accomplished work. . . . The technical control with which he told an intricate and highly articulated story, weaving back and forth from the past to the present and from Jack Kinsella's private agony to his public concerns, showed an impressive mastery of the art." Schlesinger (25) recognized the importance of the narrator to the novel and that the political story is secondary to the "fate of the family." Despite the catastrophe in the family, Schlesinger saw the novel as ending hopefully because the narrator, who had been "withdrawn and self-protective as an adult, incapable of love" because of the boyhood tragedy, finally moves toward a reconciliation with his wife and a hope for his own family. This process of maturing, of the acceptance of reality, "could perhaps produce a new strength and individuality, even perhaps a new sense of family."

Thus, the published critiques of *All in the Family* show the greatest disparity of critical reaction to any of O'Connor's novels. *All in the Family* was dismissed by some as an inferior, commercial re-write of the earlier novels or as a *roman à clef* about the Kennedys; others have claimed that this is O'Connor's best novel but, somewhere in between, though leaning toward "the best," is the judgment offered here, a judgment qualified by a distaste for making apples-and-oranges comparisons. Realistically, the critic is forced by many factors to find an oversimplified answer to the question, "What is a writer's *best* work?" This critic claims that *The Edge of Sadness* is Edwin O'Connor's most complete artistic success. *All in the Family* almost makes it, but it lacks the total sense of organic completeness of *The Edge of Sadness*.

For example, *All in the Family* lacks the depth of characterization which so distinguishes the other novel; in it, the protagonist, Father Hugh Kennedy, is fully developed and is supported by three other characters (Charlie Carmody, Father John Carmody, Father Danowski) who also receive extensive characterization. In contrast, no one other than the protagonist-narrator, Jack Kinsella, is fully developed in *All in the Family*; the supporting roles are generally one-dimensional: Charles, the opportunist; Phil, the zealot; Uncle Jimmy, the tyrant-father. Granted that one-dimensional characters, *à la* Dickens, are entertaining and often memorable, nevertheless, if one were to compare the "tyrant-fathers" of these two novels, Charlie Carmody is much more fully rendered than Uncle Jimmy. Female characterization, too, is poorly developed; albeit a general weakness in O'Connor's writing, he managed to avoid it in *The Edge of Sadness* by restricting his focus.

While some of the deliberately exaggerated auxiliary characters, such as Edso and Walshie, Mr. Guilfoyle, and others in *All in the Family* have been denounced as mere echoes of previous work, their functional roles within the story justify their delightful presence. However, in contrast, some of the melodramatic aspects (the Corrupt Political Boss and the Corrupt Contractor lurking in the background) of the political plot should have been toned down. Of greater importance, however, is the question of the final fusion and merger of themes in *All in the Family*. Although the coherence of the novel can be demonstrated by a close explication (as it is here) showing that the three separate plots are linked in the climax and dénouement, it must be recognized that this fusion is very subtle, placing great demands on the average reader. If one claims, for example as Howard Mumford Jones does, that the storyteller has a responsibility to his audience, then O'Connor owes his readers a few more obvious signs of the relationships in his final pages. O'Connor does this well in *The Edge of Sadness*, as an extensive portion of that novel—after Charlie Carmody's "deathbed" scene—focuses intently on the narrator's actions; but, in *All in the Family*, the shift back to the narrator is less extensive and less obvious.

Perhaps the explanation lies in something beyond the artist's control. Something *more* seems necessary in *All in the Family*. Perhaps this is what Kenny meant when he said that "the resolution of the impressive chords struck here seems to require, for full artistic integrity, an additional volume or volumes." On one hand, it could be argued that the narrator has achieved a "balance." Despite the problems, failures, errors and weaknesses of the past, Jack Kinsella is enduring, making do. He has an awareness of evil, without despair, and a hope, without presumption. His new family life is likely not to be built upon the illusions of a dream like Uncle Jimmy's: the authoritarian father's myth of a "happy family."

But, the narrator still holds, as an attainable ideal, the dream of a conflict-less "happy family." It will be more democratically organized, it is true, with the husband and wife on a closer-to-equal status: he does the writing, the "work," while she keeps busy with avocational dress-designing, shopping, and touring in Italy, or riding in Ireland. Not exactly a Women's Lib ideal; but, considering the starting point in the Kinsella *Kinder-Kirche-Küchen* tradidition, it indicates some progress. The ideal home life is still defined as an absence of conflict as seen in the pastoral idyllic weeks in Italy or at the Irish farmhouse. The ideal is perhaps suggested by Jack's own parents' "ideal" marriage—as he remembered it in the opening pages: total joy, no conflict, all sweetness and light. O'Connor very effectively showed the sad results of Uncle Jimmy's authoritarianism, but the "more" that is needed in the novel is Jack's awareness of the snakes that are present in his own garden of domestic paradise.

His parents, after all, weren't really that happy and gay. The illusion of happiness they created was carefully and expensively maintained for the children's sake. Eavesdropping later, in the Irish castle scene, Jack overhears his father reveal his constant fear for and his anxious watching of his wife. Jack's father, emotionally dependent on his wife's love, keeps emphasizing his great love for her. With such an intense "love" image to maintain, it is possible that Jack's father severely repressed any normal aggressions toward her. Hatred would be deeply repressed, inhibited, and intensified by his constant anxiety and frustration to prevent her "lovelessness," her lack of love-giving solace to him when she was "mad." If so, then it is conceivable that Jack's father, that day in the woods, heard his wife's ominous farewell remark as she left for the fatal canoe trip. Hearing, but in exasperation-anger-hate over his life of anxiety and "rejection," he "allowed" her to go—that is, killed her. He understood the danger; twice previously, the reader is informed of her obsessive fear of drowning, her awareness of water as being deadly.

As such, this sequence is a grand dramatization of an emotionally dependent person's "rejection" fantasy: If the lover permits the slightest "hatred" (in this case, the passive silence, an omission) against the beloved, he would be horribly punished (here, the total loss of the beloved). Afterwards, the father's subconscious guilt is overwhelming; and he confesses, almost liturgically, his guilt to a father-figure (Uncle Jimmy) who "forgives" him. Later, during the climactic argument between Phil and Charles, Jack's metaphor ("like being a spectator at a drowning"), if fully extended through that sentence, suggests a remarkable parallel between the two tragedies: "this tragedy need not come if only one of the other spectators—a particular one—would merely raise his voice or lift a finger."

Jack's father, even on his deathbed, is never able to understand the situation himself. But Jack is aware of, and has told the reader about, both the "warning sign" given by the mother and the omission by his father of this important detail when the story was told to Uncle Jimmy. These two items, plus the possible subconscious link in the "drowning" metaphor, suggest that some of the pieces of the puzzle are there. But Jack does not attempt to put them together; he allows this mystery to be left undisturbed. Some very deep currents that have been set in motion are left unresolved at the end.

It would seem very dangerous for the narrator to probe further here about his own idealized family life; he has just witnessed the destruction of the illusions of one family. So the final gesture is *tentatively* hopeful, as Schlesinger noted, qualifying it twice: "perhaps produce a new strength and individuality, even perhaps a new sense of family." But this possibility of hope seems unsupported by anything the narrator has experienced; neither Uncle Jimmy's family nor his own was really a "happy" family. Yet the narrator seems to suggest, in the face of every lesson to the contrary, that the dream is possible.

CHAPTER *10*

The Best and the Last of Edwin O'Connor

I *Death*

DEATH was sudden, unexpected. On March 23, 1968, Edwin O'Connor suffered a massive cerebral hemorrhage. He never regained consciousness, dying almost instantly. Years earlier, O'Connor had put the problem of philosophers into the whining complaint of Gottlieb, the sad Jew in *I Was Dancing*, who entered that novel dejected by the death of a friend, a man in the prime of his life who had suddenly dropped dead "from a clot on the brain." "Gentlemen," Gottlieb said, "I tell you this: a thing like that, it makes a man think. Where are we going? Why?"

In the months immediately preceding his death, O'Connor had been in an unusually buoyant and productive mood. During the previous years he had worked hard on the play, "The Traveler From Brazil," and he had been involved in the complicated and time-consuming preparation for staging it. Friends, including Arthur Thornhill, Sr., had advised him to go easy on the play and to return to the writing of fiction. Finally, he did so, and he had several novels in mind. He had planned to write one about the first-generation Irish immigrants to Boston, thus completing his cycle about the changing generations. He had also planned to write a novel about a publisher, based on the life of Arthur Thornhill, Sr. Early in 1968, however, he started to write about a Catholic cardinal; after two chapters, he left that project to begin a novel based on his own boyhood experiences. He was writing well on the "Boy" when he died.

II "The Traveler From Brazil"

"The Traveler From Brazil" is an unpublished, unproduced play written by O'Connor in 1967. Because it has not gone

[179]

through the revision process which takes place during the production of any drama, it cannot be considered as a finished piece or a final draft. But it is a complete draft of what O'Connor had in mind at least at this stage. As such it is interesting, and except for a paragraph in Schlesinger's introduction and a few notes by drama critic Elliot Norton, it is unknown.

The play opens with Gerald Caffery, a pleasant-faced man in his mid-forties, sitting alone in the outside courtyard of a small restaurant, being served iced coffee by a bartender. The whole play will take place in this one setting, which later will be revealed as the "family business," a respectable restaurant now but originally the rough saloon headquarters of Gerald's grandfather, an old-time political boss.

The "Irish" bartender, Chester Kosciusczko, speaks totally in clichés ("You give some people an inch, they'll take a mile," etc.) in answer to Gerald's loaded questions on contemporary social issues; as he controls the bartender's responses by waving him on-and-off, Gerald tells the audience (three times in a few pages) that the bartender is "Everyman" and a "spokesman for our age" and, as a "genuine fake Irishman . . . The perfect fake: the ideal symbol of everything that's happening today!" After this opening scene, the bartender does not function again until the final scene when he is suggested as an ideal "court jester" for Dr. Dentremont's institution.

After the initial dialogue with the bartender, as Gerald speaks about his family background, various characters will appear (rear stage, spotlighted) and converse with him as if in his imagination. Gerald's father, dead sixteen years—probably a suicide, appears to confess his sense of failure as a "Dad" because he had never taken Gerald fishing or to a ball game, nor did he pass on the "secrets of the Good Life" or, as "an expert in mistakes" tell the boy "how to avoid the Great Mistakes." As Gerald fondly forgives, he is interrupted by the mother's hectoring voice complaining about her husband's weaknesses: "you've been a disappointment to me since the day we were married." While the mother's voice berates her husband, Gerald's first wife, dead a year now, appears, to recall the antagonisms between her and her mother-in-law; the younger woman notes that the mother-in-law "for all her fake first-family talk, she's cold corned beef to the core," an allusion to the pretensions of the family whose money came from the shady political dealings of the grandfather. Then the grandfather, Big Charlie Doyle, appears, spotlighted alone, with the sounds of cheering crowds as he delivers a political speech urging his followers to vote "at *least* once" for him at the election tomorrow.

These imagination appearances stop as Gerald's mother, Gert, enters the cafe complaining that Gerald hasn't visited her on this her seventieth birthday. Gert is a powerful domineering old lady, the matriarch of the family, who has inherited her tribal chief position and her mannerisms from Big Charlie. This is the first matriarch in O'Connor's works (other than the "Gert" in *All in the Family* who plays a secondary role to Uncle Jimmy); as such, she is a Jimmy Kinsella with skirts, full of witty invectives. She complains of the "junk" that people have given her for her birthday and castigates her Irish friends:

We're smack in the middle of an age of miracles and wonders where I can fly on a jet to Japan and be back the same night for dinner, where everybody and his brother are running hell-bent for house lots on the moon, and how do I spend my birthday but plunked down in my living room shooting the breeze with an army of primitives who just walked in from the Potato Famine. . . . I'm up to my hips in second-hand leprechauns . . . They were all born here, they were all raised here, most of them are younger than me, yet look at them! You'd take your oath that they were born in a bog a hundred years ago and were shipped over here in a burlap bag the day before yesterday! This whole state is a paradise for chiseling stage Irishmen and they all come tumbling out of the walls on my birthday!

Gert wants to know where Gerald has been during the past year: ever since his wife's death, Gerald has been away, leaving his two children, Chrissie (nine) and Charlie (eight), with Gert at her insistence. Gerald tells his mother that he has been in Brazil and is planning to return there; as Gert keeps challenging his story, the spotlight shows several jaguar-skin clad figures—a sultry woman and two children—parodying Gert's fantasies about Gerald's life in the jungle. When his own children actually appear in the cafe, Gerald exchanges snide remarks with Gert about who is more suited to take care of them. Gerald then tells a tale, filled with exotic details of anacondas and wild animals, about Wilfred Dentremont, a rich cosmopolite who has abandoned the world to live in an idyllic spot in the Brazilian jungles.

Gerald and Gert each attempt to persuade the children to live with them: Gert points out the advantages of her wealthy situation; Gerald mocks these and paints a picture of adventure in the jungle. The argument gets bitter. Gerald sarcastically mocks his mother; she denounces him as being as bad as his father: "you've been a disappointment to me since the day you could talk! You've been the worst kind of son a woman like me could have!" As Gert gets exceedingly bitchy in one passage, a singer (rear stage) ironically counterpoints with a saccharine song, "My Mother's Eyes."

Annie Gregory, a young attractive widow, and Father Fahey, a man whose eccentric speech and actions hint that he is a bit daffy, enter the cafe seeking Gerald. Their conversation indicates that they are Gerald's associates, living at the same place as he; the talk is deliberately oblique, suggesting to the audience—and eventually to Gert—that they all reside in a rest home or asylum. The first act will close with Gert screaming that she wants to know what's going on.

But before this, the penultimate scene of the first act is a kaleidoscopic montage of spotlighted characters in the background dramatizing Gerald's angry denunciation of the idiocies of the modern world. A shaggy teen-age guitarist is the first to appear singing a pseudo-folksong in a whining voice. He is followed by a mealy-mouthed congressman who delivers a speech attacking the escalation of the Vietnam war, until a bullwhip snaps and a voice with an L.B.J. Texas twang warns him; then the congressman gives almost the same speech, but this time in favor of escalation. The next vignette has an ultraliberal clergyman enthusiastically endorsing the pretentiously mystic prattle of a drug cultist. This is followed by a hard-sell soap commercial using biblical quotations and fake testimonials from Jesus and the apostles. Then a raging black militant screams threats until a club-swinging racist sheriff removes him. Next a sweet young child unctuously does a mouthwash commercial: "My Mummy has . . . B-A-A-D BREATH! Ick! I call it . . . . . Mummytosis!" Following this, an enthusiastic announcer reads the war news, moving without transition from the casualty report to a commercial for a bathroom disinfectant. Finally, Big Charlie, delivering a few political clichés, appears in this montage, and it ends with

Gert, mouthing some platitudes, as "The Battle Hymn of the Republic" is heard in the background.

The second act takes place a week later at the same cafe. As the curtain opens, Gert is talking to a stranger who is revealed as Doctor Wilfred Dentremont. Gert has found one of Gerald's letters and has traced down Dentremont to find out about Gerald's mysterious abode. Dentremont explains that he is not a medical doctor, nor is the institution he directs a medical one. All references to the institution will be vague, but it is described in terms of a haven, an idyllic refuge for those who are weary of the world. Located only an hour away, in a pleasant isolated rural area, it is a self-contained world of its own.

When Annie, Father Fahey, and Gerald enter; the discussion about the institution continues. Gert keeps insisting that it is a "funny farm" or a "nuthouse." Dentremont tries to explain that while most people "feel uncomfortable but reconciled" to the world, some very sensitive people are always "in a state of almost continual exasperation or revulsion or rage or just plain boredom." Some of these sensitive people drop out of society; some to monasteries, some to drugs, some to Dentremont's "world" where he tries to create an atmosphere of peace. Gerald talks of the madness of the outside world, that "we've got used to it. We're addicts." Then he explains to Gert that in Dentremont's institution a few real, but harmless, lunatics such as the fake priest, Father Fahey, are there too, almost as pets for the others. Gert wonders which category Gerald and Annie belong to, and then berates Gerald for ruining the family name by his actions. Listing a whole catalogue of domestic disasters—sickness, death, deformed babies—that others in the family have stoically endured, Gert argues that Gerald is simply a weakling: "All this trashy baloney about your wonderful thin skin that's so sensitive it gets a big black bruise every time you hear about some Mick cop hitting a drunk over the head with his billyclub!"

Onstage action freezes as Gerald's satiric visions of the future world appear in the spotlighted vignettes: an eager teacher browbeats the two children to memorize a long list of esoteric facts, "college is only ten years away"; Chester, the bartender, as a "prominent layman"—a "social consultant"—has been ordained as an "Instant Padre" after a week's training and is preaching platitudes; an excited announcer reads the weekly "body count" from the war, gleeful that it is a few points below last week's count and even less than the weekend's highway death toll.

When the action resumes, Gerald asks Annie to marry him; she consents, quickly, willingly. As they recall their growing friendship at the institution, Gert violently objects to Gerald marrying "some little baggage from nowhere who's half his age and who's gone through one husband already!" A bitter argument ensues between the mother and the couple. When the children arrive, Gert and Gerald again fight over them, each trying to persuade the children to his side. Gert tries to destroy Gerald's image by revealing the Brazil story as being phony, and she tells the children that they will be unwanted nuisances once Gerald marries Annie. Gerald fights back, eventually persuading the children to join him and Annie.

Then, a reversal. Annie issues an ultimatum that she is not returning to Dentremont's institution. Dentremont encourages her to come for the sake of the children—"they would inhale happiness"—and, when this fails, he describes a newly renovated house available to them in terms of domestic appliances and conveniences, suggestive of the "suburban dream" of advertisements. Annie, who suddenly starts to project a "mother" image, concerned with "a family to bring up," rejects Dentremont's place as being unsuited for their new life.

Gerald doesn't understand. He enjoys Dentremont's isolated commune and had thought that Annie did too. He describes it as a pastoral utopia—"Ireland with amenities"—but admits, in reply to Annie's probing, that the decent people there are a little dull and make for poor conversation: "But Annie—who wants to talk?" Annie replies, "I do! I'm a human being." Granted that they're not inspiring talkers, Gerald says, *"at least they don't make any waves.* And that's the big trick today, Annie; simply to keep out of the waves! If you don't—you drown!" Annie replies that she is not going to live any more behind Dentremont's dike which holds back the waves, because the people who are happy there are happy in a creepy sort of a way; they're vegetables. Annie's ultimatum is final; she will marry Gerald only if he chooses some other, any other, place to live.

Now, Gert, seeing a possibility of splitting the couple, reverses herself and starts praising the benefits of Dentremont's place. As Dentremont reminds Gerald of the horrors of the outside world, an abbreviated version of the spotlighted montage (guitarist, commercials, announcers) appears backstage.

Caught between opposing forces, Gerald is forced to a decision crisis, the apparent climax of the play. Dentremont, Gert, and Gerald's own horror of the outside world favor his return to Dentremont's institution, the imaginary Brazil of his tales; but, if he returns, he will lose Annie. Calling his children to him, Gerald reminds them of his earlier promise that early one *morning* he would awaken them at *home* and take them to Brazil. Now, he says, it is an *afternoon*, at grandma's saloon, so "when you find yourself in a situation like this, there's just one thing you can do . . . you *compromise.*" What does that word mean, they ask. A million meanings, he replies, but "it *always* means: 'I don't care what the rest may do, but we're on our way to Brazil!' "

Which Brazil, asks Annie. Gerald says "the other one . . . in South America." Joyfully, Annie joins him and the children. Gert says they'll starve. Annie asks what *will* they do, and Gerald replies casually that they can do all sorts of things, "We may breed parrots. We may start an anaconda ranch." (Joyous exuberance or madness?) The family goes off to celebrate. Gert and Dentremont are left onstage to talk briefly. The play ends with Dentremont, who senses the bartender's usefulness as a daffy decoration for his institution, inviting Chester to work for him.

Schlesinger, in summarizing the play (27), stated: "One feels that marriage had accelerated his process of self-exploration and self-knowledge. His growing ability to portray young women showed itself again in the play. . . . Eventually one of O'Connor's best female characters appears to draw Gerald back to life. She persuades him to accept reality, and they go off to the real Brazil. The play, with streaks of satire and sadness, is both funny and desperate. Unfortunately it does not lend itself to excerpts."

Elliot Norton, a Boston drama critic and close friend of O'Connor, added some background information on the production problems of the play; in Norton's *Record American* column (March 6, 1970) he reported that the play had first been sent to David Merrick, who had produced *I Was Dancing*, and had been returned without comment. Then, "Leland Hayward took it under option and submitted it to Henry Fonda, who, for a time, considered playing the title role. Hayward finally dropped the option, because, he said, the play 'needs work'; it is not playable in its present form, and he 'would not put it into rehearsal until he could get a playwright—acceptable to Veniette O'Connor, the author's widow, to work on it.'

Commenting on the play itself, Norton saw Gert as "a new kind of O'Connor character, a tough-minded possessive mother." He noted that the battle between the mother and the girl was "theatrically traditional with roots back as far as Sidney Howard's *The Silver Cord*" and that the imaginary characters under the spotlights were reminiscent of the technique used by Miller in *Death of a Salesman*. After praising the delightful irony in the dialogue, Norton concluded that O'Connor was a "great American novelist who found the theater attractive but never quite mastered its techniques."

Some problems of characterization and plotting could probably be revised by a competent "play doctor." For example, Annie's decision to leave security, and her *post facto* reasoning, is simply asserted, not adequately explained or motivated by her previous actions; until the moment of her surprising announcement, she too had been a voluntary resident at Dentremont's place and relatively quiet within the play. In plotting, there is difficulty with the pace and the suspense interest of the conflicts: Act One ends with only a *mild* problem unsolved; an audience might be curious but hardly very concerned; when a major conflict occurs (Gerald's decision), the resolution is too fast, and rather expected. Other problem areas are debatable: one could object that the children are mere puppets onstage, but such flatness of characterization of minor parts can be dramatically justified; or one could point out that Gerald's adequate financial situation effectively shields him from real pressures here: he is as solvent and as footloose as any of Henry James' jobless heroes.

However, the major weakness of the play does not rest in any of the details, nor can it be "corrected" by others. Essentially there is a confusion between two themes: one is of a personal nature, a family problem; the other is a morality play about "dropping out" of a corrupt society. Because O'Connor's real interest seems to be in the first theme—in Gerald's triumph over his mother's wishes—the implications of his decision to go to

Brazil leave the second theme unresolved. While Gerald's's "compromise" to go to Brazil is an effective victory over his mother, who was then pressing him to go to Dentremont's, it is *not* a decision to face the realities of the outside world. Gerald is not taking his family to the *real* Brazil of poverty in the barrios, political unrest and repression, and gross social inequities; he is taking them to a Brazil of "anacondas and bananas," a pleasant, spacious, outdoor zoo, a tropical paradise. By substituting a different haven, this "compromise" does not resolve the conflict between social involvement and alienation; it is merely a temporary delaying action or diversion. Once in Brazil, the decision would have to be confronted again—whether to withdraw and to isolate oneself in a vegetable kingdom or to live involved in the imperfect society of man.

O'Connor shouldn't be damned for not presenting mankind with the "Answer" to this dilemma; on the other hand, this play should not be reckoned as a sufficiently developed, serious exploration of the alienation theme. Although the play is sprinkled with topical allusions to contemporary problems, this oversimplification ("going to Brazil") of social issues seems straight out of the drama of the thirties, just as some of the theatrical devices (symbolic bartenders) seem to come from early O'Neill. Viewed in a wider context, O'Connor seems to be showing his age, reflecting the basically optimistic liberalism of his generation; younger writers, in younger media, are less hopeful about even the possibility of such utopian retreats. For example, in the movie *Alice's Restaurant*, Ray's earnest search for an idyllic commune is seen as futile by Arlo whose wistful shrug at the end suggests that the alienated young are too unbelieving in such utopian dreams even to be surprised or disillusioned at their failure.

III *The Best and the Last of Edwin O'Connor*

After O'Connor's death, three major projects were suggested by his friends at the *Atlantic* office as a means of sustaining interest in his work. The first of these plans was to edit some of the tape recordings previously made by O'Connor reading from his own works (see bibliography). The second idea was to find someone to work on and revise the unpublished play, "The Traveler From Brazil"; for various reasons, this plan was not carried out. The third project was the publication of a post-humous collection, a "sampler" of some of O'Connor's best published work, together with some previously unpublished material, and some related memoirs.

By late 1968, the various plans for a posthumous book had been weighed; Mrs. Esther Yntema, senior editor who had worked closely with O'Connor for almost twenty years, was in charge of the book and suggested following a rigorous critical principle that only O'Connor's finished work would be collected. Thus, "The Traveler From Brazil," the unpublished play manuscript, was omitted because it needed revision. "The Cardinal" fragment and "The Boy" fragment were to be included, however, on the basis that these parts of the proposed novels were "finished" as far as O'Connor was concerned.

In the years after *The Last Hurrah*, O'Connor's attention to style increased to the point where he would labor over a single word or sentence meticulously until it suited him. For example, the handwritten notebooks used for "The Cardinal" have thirty-three different versions, written on individual sheets, of the two sentences which appear in the final version (412) as: "The experience had been unsettling. Partly—he later realized—because of the coincidence: on that very day he had been thinking a great deal about old age." Once such a "problem" sentence had been solved, O'Connor worked at the typewriter. Whenever he finished a page, it was a final draft: clean, free from errors, strikeovers, emendations; for he would never return to the page again. But, in the process of achieving this final draft, O'Connor accumulated reams of pages half-typed, or with one minor typing error, discarded as he began typing the whole page over again. It was a slow process, but once a page was completed, it never needed revision either by O'Connor or by his editors. Nor would he tolerate revisions by others; although he could "take editing" if suggested verbally to him before a work was completed, once done his work was his own. The *Benjy* manuscript, for example, has one red-pencil correction on it, made by an editor suggesting a change in verb form; this notation has been partially erased and in the margin O'Connor wrote a large, emphatic "NO!"

After the decision to publish had been made, the historian Arthur Schlesinger, Jr., was invited to edit and to write the introduction. Schlesinger, whose distinguished career in writing and in politics gave him the background to assess O'Connor, was an ideal choice because he had also been a close friend and would be able to write a unique personal memoir. Of special interest in the Schlesinger introduction is the collection of letters which O'Connor wrote, in various *personae*, to his friends; the high-spirited humor and droll wit in them effectively suggest the easy informality of his friendships. Schlesinger's description of the literary community at Wellfleet; his brief, but penetrating, analyses of the novels; his treatment of O'Connor as a novelist of manners; and his lyrical tribute to O'Connor's personal qualities are all important contributions to the understanding of the writer.

One of the previously unpublished pieces gathered for this new collection was the fragment of an intended novel, "The Great Baldini," written in collaboration with the literary critic, Edmund Wilson. The *Atlantic* of November, 1969, published this fragment in advance of the release of *The Best and the Last of Edwin O'Connor* and with Wilson's recollections of his friendship with O'Connor. From the evidence in "The Great Baldini" and from the testimony of his friends who recalled his constant playfulness with card tricks and "passes," it might be useful to think of O'Connor, *the writer*, as a magician. Metaphorically, "O'Connor, the Magician" might suggest not only some of his recurrent themes of illusion and reality, delusion of others and self-delusion, but also O'Connor's skill in attracting the reader's attention with one hand while working his magic with the other. While the reader is being entertained and distracted watching the flamboyant actions of Charlie Carmody in *The Edge of Sadness* or Jimmy Kinsella in *All in the Family*, O'Connor is subtly using his other hand to work the magic with the main characters of those two novels, the narrators. There is no evidence that O'Connor ever deliberately or consciously structured the novels in this way, but this analogy suggests that, when a person's lifetime hobby is concerned with feints, sleight of hand, and deliberate distractions, some of these techniques may very naturally appear in his writings. Certainly such evasive tricks would complement the rambling storytelling techniques of detours and digressions of which O'Connor was conscious.

Although Wilson's remembrances of O'Connor were not intended as a formal critique, he does make a few critical estimates

in his opening memoir. He notes that O'Connor's popular success with *The Last Hurrah* caused most literary critics to ignore
the later books. Generally, Wilson praises O'Connor's writing,
especially noting the richness of characterization and dialogue;
his one negative comment focuses on O'Connor's digressive storytelling: "His one dramatic weakness, which he was trying to over-
come, was his tendency to prolong conversations, making them
loop around and around without satisfactorily progressing. This,
I think, was his chief difficulty in writing plays, in which a
dialogue must not go on too long and must take steps to arrive
at some destination." Two important points can be deduced from
this comment: first, O'Connor *recognized* his habitual digressive
technique and saw it as a *dramatic* weakness; second, the technique may be a flaw in the drama—where the genre has severe
limits on time and space—but it is not necessarily a flaw in the
novel, or around the family dinner table, where such open-ended
conversations are common. Here, such digressions are tolerated
and encouraged because of the accumulating layers of story and
of characterization which can develop.

The fragment of "The Cardinal" is akin in spirit and in several
literary devices to the opening section of *The Last Hurrah*. Again,
the protagonist is a public figure, a tribal chieftain, at the end of
his career. The story begins on the evening of the Golden Jubilee
celebrating the cardinal's fifty years as a priest. He recollects the
events of the day in a panoramic survey of the visits, interviews,
banquets. From these brief scenes, the cardinal is portrayed as a
lover of "the City," (just as Skeffington—and O'Connor—loved
"the City") and as a legendary figure, especially according to the
exaggerated newspaper accounts of his life. The writing is rich
and full-bodied, O'Connor's mature style; and this collection of
incidents serves to illuminate not only the inner life of the cardinal but also the external changes in the Church.

The final work in the collection is "The Boy" fragment, the
novel on which O'Connor was working at his death; and it is
published exactly as O'Connor left it, ending in mid-sentence.
(In contrast, when excerpts from "The Boy" were published in
McCall's [February, 1970, 90ff.] under *their* title, "The Magic
Man," this version was severely edited and rearranged.) "The
Boy," a rich story, draws on O'Connor's own memories of boy-
hood and interweaves a complex cast of characters into what

probably would have been a suspense story because several early foreshadowings hint at the possible complications.

IV   Conclusion

If quality of mind, complexity of vision, and control of presentation are desirable qualities, then critics who ignore the major writings of Edwin O'Connor, or blandly parrot the gross errors of some of the early reviewers, do a disservice to the intellectual life. This book has been offered as a "corrective introduction" to clear away some of the critical debris which has obscured O'Connor's reputation in some quarters, especially among the academic critics. To refute the charges of "commercialism" and "exploitation," the circumstances of his life and the testimony of his friends (rather distinguished and discriminating men) have been presented as "character witnesses." Although O'Connor in person needed no such outside aid, the scholar of the future who perhaps reads the "Kennedy" reviews of *All in the Family* ought to know of O'Connor's integrity as a writer and as a person. To refute the charges that O'Connor's stories rambled off on meaningless side-tracks, an extensive explication of the novels has been offered to show the relationship and coherence of the parts of his intricate stories. To refute that old charge of "popularity"—as if a wide audience meant *ipso facto* some kind of pandering—one can only defend the novelist's role as storyteller, as John Steinbeck did in his Nobel Prize speech: "Literature was not promulgated by a pale and emasculated critical priesthood singing their litanies in empty churches—nor is it a game for the cloistered elect, the tin-horn mendicants of low-calorie despair."

In a more positive way, this study has suggested O'Connor's achievement as a novelist, his ability to tell stories of great interest and meaning, to people them with memorable characters, and to write sustained, vigorous prose and delightful dialogue. He is, as Howard Mumford Jones claimed, a "proper heir" to the great tradition of the novel. Despite the technical limitations of the novel, *The Last Hurrah* will outlive scores of its more stylish contemporaries and will retain its vigor and freshness; Frank Skeffington will remain as one of the great characters in modern American writing. *The Edge of Sadness*, in addition to its historical importance as being the first realistic priest-novel, marking the maturity of religious literature within American Catholicism, is a most distinguished example of technical achievement in its narrative persona and in its structure. And *All in the Family* is a remarkable attempt in O'Connor's "detour" style of storytelling, interweaving intricate inner dramas with external ones.

As Schlesinger (11) reported, O'Connor once told a friend, "I would like to do for the Irish in America what Faulkner did for the South." In his later work, O'Connor was moving toward this goal by adding layer upon layer in density as he portrayed the complexities of the changing generations in their environments of Church, family, and politics. Underlying this seriousness of purpose, O'Connor's sense of wit and humor gave a special warmth to his writing. At ease with his Irish-American material, he was both well-informed and detached, both skeptical and tolerant, fully aware of both the good and the bad within a group or within a man, and O'Connor's complexity has frustrated some of his critics.

But, despite O'Connor's accomplishments in dealing with his Irish-American material, it would not be correct to see him simply as an ethnic writer. As the scholar, Daniel Aaron, in *America* (May 4, 1968, 604), has said: "It would be wrong, however, to see him primarily as a local-colorist capitalizing on their quaint and idiosyncratic behavior. Social historians in time will appreciate how perceptively O'Connor documents the acculturation of the Boston Irish . . . but he is no more a 'hyphenate' or ethnic writer than are Saul Bellow or Ralph Ellison. He neither looks out from behind a minority barricade nor represents himself as the conscious exponent of an ethnic group. Rather he is akin to those contemporary American novelists whose race or ethnic origin merely provides color for their fictive pallettes, writers who happen to be Jews or Negroes or Irish Catholics, but who have moved from a parochial sphere into a universal one."

Selected Bibliography

PRIMARY SOURCES

1. *Books*
The Oracle. New York: Harper & Bros., 1951.
The Last Hurrah. Boston: Atlantic-Little, Brown, 1956.
Benjy: A Ferocious Fairy Tale. Boston: Atlantic-Little, Brown, 1957.
The Edge of Sadness. Boston: Atlantic-Little, Brown, 1961.
I Was Dancing. Boston: Atlantic-Little, Brown, 1964.
The Best and the Last of Edwin O'Connor. Boston: Atlantic-Little,
    Brown, 1970. Posthumous collection. Edited with an introduction
    by Arthur Schlesinger, Jr.

2. *Short Stories*
(Chapter Two gives a full listing of published *articles* and *unpublished*
short stories.)

"The Gentle, Perfect Knight." *Atlantic,* 180 (September, 1947), 59–63.
"The Inner Self." *Atlantic,* 185 (April, 1950), 64–68.
"Parish Reunion." *The Yale Review,* 40 (September, 1950), 59–69.
"A Grand Day for Mr. Garvey." *Atlantic,* 200 (October, 1957), 46–50.

3. *Manuscripts*
The O'Connor manuscripts are currently in the Little, Brown archives
in Boston; the notebooks have been retained by his widow. Eventually, all materials will be deposited in the Boston Public Library.

4. *Recordings*
In 1969, CMS Records (14 Warren St., New York) released two LP
records of O'Connor reading selections from *The Last Hurrah* (CMS
#574)—Skeffington's speech at the Eddie McLaughlin memorial din-
ner, "Mother" Garvey's visit with Charlie Hennessey, and portions of
Skeffington's deathbed reverie; and from *The Edge of Sadness* (CMS
#578)—Father Kennedy's description of St. Paul's neighborhood, and
a scene with Father Danowski. Both records demonstrate O'Connor's
ability as a speaker and mimic, but of special interest is O'Connor's
own conception of Skeffington's speech.

SECONDARY SOURCES

Reviews of individual novels are cited within the appropriate chapter.
Reference data has been incorporated within the text itself.

BLOTNER, JOSEPH. *The Modern American Political Novel.* (Austin: University of Texas Press, 1966), includes only a brief analysis of *The Last Hurrah,* but it contains extensive information about the wider context of political novels, themes, and archetypal characters.

CURLEY, JAMES MICHAEL. *I'd Do It Again!* (Englewood Cliffs, N.J.: Prentice-Hall, 1957), is the autobiography of Boston's mayor. It contains useful comparisons and contrasts regarding the character of Skeffington.

JONES, HOWARD MUMFORD. "Politics, Mr. O'Connor, and the Family Novel." *Atlantic,* 218 (October, 1966), 117–19, is an extended review of *All in the Family* in the context of political and family novels. It places O'Connor in the "great tradition" of the novelist as storyteller.

KELLEHER, JOHN V. "Edwin O'Connor and the Irish American Process." *Atlantic,* 222 (July, 1968), 48–52, is a personal memoir of a Harvard professor of Irish literature in which he records his friendship with O'Connor and gives an analysis of O'Connor's rendering of the Irish-American experience.

MILNE, GORDON. *The American Political Novel.* Norman: University of Oklahoma Press, 1966. (See pp. 153–179, "Professionals: Warren, O'Connor, and Drury.")

RANK, HUGH. "O'Connor's Image of the Priest." *New England Quarterly,* 41 (March, 1968), 3–29, is an analysis of *The Edge of Sadness* in the context of Catholic literature and the priest-novel. It was originally a chapter from a dissertation: "The Changing Image of the Priest in American Catholic Fiction," University of Notre Dame, 1969.

SCHLESINGER, ARTHUR M., JR. "Introduction" to *The Best and the Last of Edwin O'Connor.* Boston: Atlantic-Little, Brown, 1970, is a thirty-two-page memoir and analysis, and is the most important article to complement this present book.

SHANNON, WILLIAM V. *The American Irish.* New York: Macmillan, 1963, is an informed, wide-ranging study of the diverse aspects of the Irish experience in American politics, literature, and culture.

WILSON, EDMUND. "The Great Baldini: A Memoir and a Collaboration by Edmund Wilson and Edwin O'Connor." *Atlantic,* 224 (October, 1969), 64–75. Reprinted in *The Best and the Last of Edwin O'Connor,* pp. 341–367. This is a long memoir by the famous critic, and a fragment of an intended novel for which Wilson and O'Connor were playfully writing alternate chapters.

Index

PS3565
C55Z85   Rank, Hugh.

C48345

Edwin O'Connor. New York, Twayne Publishers ₁1974₁

197 p. port. 21 cm. (Twayne's United States authors series,
TUSAS 242)

Bibliography: p. 193–194.

1. O'Connor, Edwin.

PS3565.C55Z85
ISBN 0–8057–0555–4

813'.5'4

73–17301
MARC

Library of Congress

74 ₁4₁